D0558811

SOCIALLY ELECTED

SOCIALLY ELECTED

How To Win Elections Using Social Media

Craig Agranoff and Herbert Tabin

Copyright © 2011 Craig Agranoff and Herbert Tabin

Published By Pendant Publishing — www.pendantpublishing.net

Copy Editor: Genevieve V. DeGuzman

Book Designer and Compositor: Rosamond Grupp

ISBN: 978-0-578-09216-4

Printing History

First Edition: August 2011

While every precaution has been taken in preparing this book, the publisher and author assume no responsibility for errors and omissions, or for damages resulting from the use of the information contained herein. Technology and services are constantly changing and therefore might contain errors and/or information that, while accurate when it was written, may be no longer accurate by the time you read it. Your use of or reliance on the information in this book is at your own risk and the author and Pendant Publishing disclaim and responsibility for any resulting damage or expense. The content of this book represents the views of the authors only, and does not represent the views of Pendant Publishing.

Notice of Rights

All rights reserved. No part of this book may be reproduced or transmitted in any form by any means, electronic, mechanical, photocopying, recording, or otherwise, without the prior written permission of the publisher. For information on getting permission for reprints and excerpts, contact info@pendantpublishing.net.

Notice of Liability

The information in this book is distributed on an "As Is" basis without warranty. While every precaution has been taken in the preparation of the book, neither the authors nor Pendant Publishing shall have any liability to any person or entity with respect to any loss or damage caused or alleged to be caused directly or indirectly by the instructions contained in this book or by the computer software and hardware products described in it.

Trademarks

Many of the designations used by manufacturers and sellers to distinguish their products are claimed as trademarks. Where those designations appear in this book, and Pendant Publishing was aware of a trademark claim, the designations appear as requested by the owner of the trademark. All other product names and services identified throughout this book are used in an editorial fashion only and for the benefit of such companies with no intention of infringement of the trademark. No such use, or the use of any trade name, is intended to convey endorsement or other affiliation with this book.

About The Authors

Craig Agranoff is the CBS Television News tech correspondent for the CBS12 evening news, CBS Radio103.1, and Co-Founder of Gripd. com an interactive agency. He is an entrepreneur, and national Social Engagement consultant, as well as a noted specialist in location based online marketing. He is the author of *Do It Yourself Online Reputation Management: A Step-By-Step Guide to Building or Repairing Your Online Reputation* and *CheckedIn: How To Use Gowalla Foursquare and Other Geo Location Applications For Fun and Profit.* He recently won a Digital PR award for his work with Chevrolet. He also was a Tech/Social Media Correspondent in the *New Times, Palm Beach Post*, and *VentureBeat*.com. Currently he is a Tech Columnist for *Miami Living Magazine* and *The Huffington Post.* Craig has been featured in the *Miami Herald, Newsday, The BBC,* The Street.com, *New Times, The Palm Beach Post, AOL Digital Cities, Slice, CenterNetworks, Thrillist* and *The Sun-Sentinel.* Craig also has appeared on Gary Vaynerchuck's Wine Library TV, Fox News, NBC News and CBS News.

Herbert Tabin is the CBS Television News tech correspondent for the CBS12 evening news, CBS Radio103.1 as well as an author, investment banker, entrepreneur, venture capitalist, merger and acquisition expert and noted specialist in online reputation management and monitoring. He is the author of *Do It Yourself Online Reputation Management: A Step-By-Step Guide to Building or Repairing Your Online Reputation* and *CheckedIn: How To Use Gowalla Foursquare and Other Geo Location Applications For Fun and Profit.* He has worked with many Internet startups, the blog sCommerce.com and operated Rev2.org. Tabin has been featured on the cover of *Entrepreneur Magazine* (Entrepreneurs Business Start-Ups), *The Palm Beach Post, Newsday, The BBC,* The Street.com and in Steve Spalding's book, *All the Little Things – Get* *the advice you will need to get your idea out of the garage and onto the web.* He is a frequent speaker at technology events. Over the years he has received various entrepreneurial award nominations including Ernst and Young's Entrepreneur of the Year Award, received The Award for Business Leadership. He was also nominated as a finalist for best Large Scale Social Network, winning best "Photo Sharing Website Category" at Mashable's Open Web Awards. In March 2000, the State University of New York At Oneonta named its largest computer lab, the 'Tabin Computer Lab'.

Contents

Chapter 1

Why Social Media Matters

THE USE of social media and political purposes isn't entirely new. Many argue that Thomas Paine's political tract, *Common Sense*, was an early example of social media in action, galvanizing people in town halls and taverns. Today, blogs, Facebook, Twitter, and other social media platforms are being used to organize movements and amass volunteers for various campaigns at local and national levels. Facebook alone has more than 700 million active users worldwide, and surpasses even Google in page views.[1] At heart of the social revolution in politics today is the scale and accessibility of the technology that undergirds it. Different from the past, political campaigns, both local and national, can now propel candidates into office by banking on social media's vast infrastructure.

To witness the current power of social media and the Internet's influence on today's politics you don't need to go any further than Iceland. In June 2011, the tiny Nordic country, was undergoing a massive overhaul

---

1   "Facebook: Now 700 Million Strong?", 31 May 2011, *Business Insider*, http://www. businessinsider.com/facebook-700-million-2011-5 (accessed 15 June 2011).

in its government in the wake of economic catastrophe. What's different though, is that it plans to use crowdsourcing to draft a revamped constitution.[2] Iceland's government will marshal social media to source proposals and opinions from its people through various social networking channels. The constitutional council will be posting draft clauses on its website and will be asking the public to comment on its Facebook page. Meetings are already being streamed live on both places. In essence, the citizens of Iceland will see the constitution develop right before their eyes and will have a hand in seeing it come to fruition.

Iceland's digital experiment is a fitting analogy of the way politics is run today. Campaigns are no longer the machinations of a few insiders, out of sight and out of touch with the public. With social media, campaigns are now very much in the public eye— demanding a presence on various platforms, such as Twitter, YouTube, Facebook, and Flickr.

While Iceland's constitution demonstrates one use of social media, a look on the other side of the world, shows a very different influence of how social media tools are being championed. In the Arab world social media is being used as the weapons of an Arab Spring fomenting revolution and revolutionary waves across Tunisia, Egypt, Syria, Bahrain, and Libya among others brought on by ordinary citizens to topple dictators. In Egypt, Facebook pages memorializing fallen citizens are rallying millions of fans.

All these monumental changes brought on by a new technology, many regarded as a toy, leave many asking "how did we get here"? To answer that question we have to look no further back to 2008 when Barack Obama's official and unofficial social networks arguably propelled him to election victory and the White House in 2008. It was hard

---

2 "Iceland crowdsources its next constitution", 10 June 2011, *The Washington Post* blog, http://www.washingtonpost.com/blogs/blogpost/post/iceland-crowdsources-its-next-constitution/2011/06/10/AGiBplOH_blog.html (accessed 15 June 2011).

to imagine that just a year before, when Obama announced his candidacy, he was considered a long shot for the presidency by many counts: He lacked the depth of experience on the national and international stage held by his opponents. Outside of Illinois, he was relatively unknown and he was also up against one of the biggest political machines of all time— the Clintons, who were regarded by many as the embodiment of the Democratic Party with far-reaching influence and deep pockets to mount a formidable campaign.

So how did a lightweight win the presidency against all odds? Through a political campaign that harnessed social media in new and creative ways. While Obama's 2008 run will be a hard act to follow, already opponents in the 2012 presidential election are mounting their own campaigns grounded in social media tactics.

Already Republican Tim Pawlenty announced his bid to run on Facebook. Mitt Romney and Newt Gingrich did it on Twitter, with less than 140 characters. Even President Barack Obama, hard-pressed to replicate the well-oiled social media machine of 2008, kicked off his re-election bid with a YouTube video sent out to his millions of supporters.

So what part does social media play in your campaign? Do you know what's needed to win in todays election scene? Are you willing to adapt? All-in-all the rules to winning elections have officially changed. As a candidate you can either choose to embrace the new rules surrounding the ballot box or simply plan defeat. Social media is now the game changer. It's this easy to understand, as a candidate you can either stay ahead of the curve utilizing social tools or fall way behind it, the choice is yours.

Social Media: The Game Changer For Winning Elections

There are six primary reasons that social media has become an integral part of political campaigns:

- **Social media reaches and connects people.**

- **Social media accelerates how information is spread.**

- **Social media has become an integral part of how people live.**

- **Savvy campaign strategists can use social media to connect targeted demographics with customized messaging.**

- **Social media decentralizes campaign efforts— and makes it easier to mobilize small groups in different places at once.**

- **Social media makes it safe to express support or dissent.**

Social media reaches and connects people.

What social media enables every voter to do is to participate and feel connected to a campaign. It makes regular people feel part of the process. In Obama's 2008 campaign, ordinary citizens responded to the sense of ownership— feeling as if they were contributing to the momentum of a movement— something that would in the past had been reserved for lobby groups and the big donors cutting big checks.

Social media, in essence, cultivates a sense of infectious enthusiasm that can be harnessed for an organized purpose. Campaigns have new platforms to circulate and disseminate updates, issues, and campaign news on social networks, blogs, and e-mail— making civic participation in the political process an exciting, fresh experience again. Everyday, ordinary citizens can reach the candidates in direct ways through social networks. Simply put— it brings politicians closer to the people. Campaigns use social networks to reach more people and to strengthen their relationship with supporters at a wider level.

Social media accelerates how information is spread.

In the digital space where social media resides, ideas can be spread quickly and virally—mobilizing groups of people faster. In this dynamic digital environment, information— beneficial and harmful— spreads and encircles communities quickly as users upload information to their social networking accounts, and primary, secondary, and tertiary levels of friends 'pass the word along'. Social media users share video, photos, and other content with such immediacy that campaigns no longer need to use traditional media outlets to get the news out. With access to social media tools on the Internet, every person becomes a potential media outlet.

Social media has become an integral part of how people live.

The goal is to reach voters in the social media spaces where they already converse, interact and socialize. On social media sites, we rant and rave, we shop, we conduct business, and we stay connected with friends and family. Social media allows political campaigns to reach, energize, and galvanize supporters regardless of where they are and allows political candidates to connect with potential voters online where they interact, guiding them to their campaign.

Savvy campaign strategists can use social media to connect targeted demographics with customized messaging—

encouraging actions that achieve a wide range of campaign objectives. For example, the Obama 2008 campaign emphasized content that was relevant to the group being targeted. On GLEE, an online site for proud gays and lesbians, Obama highlighted his stance on promoting equality. For his Faith-based followers, he tweaked the message to focus on his religious beliefs and faith.

Social media decentralizes campaign efforts— and makes it easier to mobilize small groups in different places at once.

Tactically, social media can be used offensively and defensively by allowing campaigns to maneuver and strategize events and rallies easily. An invitation to attend a rally to support a candidate or to organize a 'flash mob' to disrupt an opponent's event can spread virally through mobile devices linked to social networks, such as Facebook, Twitter, and Foursquare. In this way, fringe movements can create 'tipping points' that can sway a campaign one way or another. While authorities and campaign security teams can restrict traditional media, any ordinary citizen attending a rally with a mobile phone camera can take a video and upload it to the Internet— either helping or hurting a campaign depending on the circumstances.

Social media makes it safe to express support or dissent.

In many ways, social media creates 'safe spaces' where people can voice their agreement and disagreement, connecting with others who share the same sentiments. As a result, people can easily 'jump on the bandwagon', going from being lukewarm supporters or dissenters to stalwart supporters or active protestors.

In traditional campaigns, only a handful of very wealthy donors are recognized for their efforts. A donation of $5 to a campaign isn't much cause for celebration. But with online networks, that $5 becomes a badge of courage— a milestone to be shared on Facebook or Twitter. You can announce that you contributed to a particular campaign on your Facebook status and Twitter stream. Indicating your participation in an activity with your friends becomes a badge of political fraternity with your social network. This virtual politicking can easily embolden people to engage in more full-throttle, on-the-ground political activity.

With increasing activity on blogs, wikis, media-sharing sites, social networking sites, and online communities— ignoring social media puts your social media campaign at risk. Now more than ever, mounting a sophisticated political campaign means not only mastering social media channels, but also harnessing social media in strategic ways.

Chapter 2

Statistics and Trends: Why Social Media Wins Campaigns

IF YOU want to win an election in the digital age, you need to go where the people are— online.

Social media for political uses is growing at a furious pace as people are starting to turn to social media for solid information, which has enormous potential that can be harnessed by political campaigns. The Obama camp in the 2008 presidential elections mobilized millions through a Facebook campaign, utilized YouTube and Twitter to ignite energy among constituents, attracted voter attention, and rode a political wave that propelled him to the White House. In contrast to 2008 in which Democrats used online social networks to incite their base, 2010 saw Republican voters and Tea Party supporters using these outlets to get their messages out. Both parties are now using social media aggressively in their campaigns.

In the run-off for the Republican 2012 primary election, GOP candidates are already mobilizing to use social media tools. In response to

Obama's "Are You In?" YouTube videos, Tim Pawlenty, the ex-governor of Minnesota responded with his own YouTube video boldly calling for a new direction for America against the failures of the Obama administration. Announcements to run are breaking out on Twitter feeds. Newt Gingrich made his announcement on Twitter. Despite his foray into social media, the number of Facebook fans and followers still falls far behind Obama. Pawlenty only has 81,000 Facebook fans so far— easily dwarfed by Obama's 19 million, accumulated since 2008.[3] The nearest conservative in terms of Facebook fans is Sarah Palin, the darling of the Tea Party, with over 2 million supporters on the social media site.

Bob Ivins, vice president of comScore, points to the increasing activity on social networking sites. "Literally hundreds of millions of people around the world are visiting social networking sites each month and many are doing so on a daily basis. It would appear that social networking is not a fad but rather an activity that is being woven into the very fabric of the global Internet."[4]

The social networking numbers are real and their impact is what makes them critical components of any political campaign. Let's take a look at the 2008 presidential campaign fight.

At the end of the campaign period, McCain's Facebook supporters numbered at 620,359, behind Obama' s 2,379,102 supporters.[5] Similar

3   "President Obama the Life of the Social Medi Party for 2012 Election", 6 April 2011, http://communication-solutions.tmcnet.com/topics/communication-solutions/articles/161773-president-obama-life-the-social-media-party-2012.htm (accessed 15 June 2011).

4   comScore Press Release, 31 July 2007 http://www.comscore.com/Press_Events/Press_Releases/2007/07/Social_Networking_Goes_Global/%28language%29/eng-US, (accessed 15 June 2011).

5   "How Obama Won Using Digital and Social Media", http://www.slideshare.net/james.burnes/how-obama-won-using-digital-and-social-media-presentation (accessed 15 June 2011).

discrepancies in social network presence existed on MySpace and Twitter. On MySpace, Obama sported 833,151 supporters compared to McCain's 217,811; on Twitter, Obama had 113,474 followers as opposed to McCain's 4,603.[6] Overall, Obama had 5 million supporters on various social networking sites in 2008.

On YouTube, Obama's 2008 campaign channel had nearly 1,800 'official' videos posted, 18,413,110 channel views, and boasted a subscribership that was four times larger than the subscribership for the McCain campaign's channel, which only had 300 'official' videos and 2,032,993 channel views. In particular, Obama's "Yes We Can" music video garnered more than 14.2 million views. Overall, the winning campaign produced officially and unofficially (from supporters, but outside of the campaign's directive) over 14.7 million hours of video footage in 2008.

On its homegrown social network at MyBarackObama.com, more than 2 million people created personal profiles, planning over 200,000 offline events for fundraising and outreach. More than half a million blog posts were written. Members were also able to create their own personal fundraising pages, which drew more than 70,000 users and raised $30 million. In the social media arena, Obama's campaign easily trounced McCain's by a 3 to 1 margin across all platforms. According to Arianna Huffington, of *The Huffington Post*, "Were it not for the Internet, Barack Obama would not be president. Were it not for the Internet, Barack Obama would not have been the nominee."[7]

---

6   "Snapshot of Presidential Candidate Social Networking Stats: Nov. 3, 2008", http://www.web-strategist.com/blog/2008/11/03/snapshot-of-presidential-candidate-social-networking-stats-nov-2-2008/ (accessed 15 June 2011).

7   "How Obama's Internet Campaign Changed Politics", 7 November 2008, The New York Times, http://bits.blogs.nytimes.com/2008/11/07/how-obamas-Internet-campaign-changed-politics/ (accessed 15 June 2011).

Key Trends Campaigns Should Watch

There are several trends supporting why social media is critical to winning a campaign:

More people are getting their information over the Internet. Overall, Internet traffic is expected to increase four-fold by 2015 driven by: the increasing number of networked devices on the market, such as tablets, smartphones, and mobile computing devices, which is expected to reach 15 billion in four years; the sheer number of people who are connected online (about 40 percent of the world population); and the increase in user content (about a million video minutes— more than two years of footage) populating Internet traffic.[8] Spending on social media marketing is expected to reach $3.1 billion by 2014, according Forrester Research— rapidly growing at a compound annual growth rate of nearly 34 percent.[9]

According to the comScore *2010 U.S. Digital Year in Review* and *2010 Data Passport,* more than 90 percent of Internet users in the U.S. have visited a social networking site at least once in a month, with the average Internet user spending almost five hours on these sites.[10] The report also cites that 14.4 percent of any time spent on the web is devoted to social media and networking online.

---

8   "Global Internet Traffic Projected to Quadruple by 2015", 1 June 2011, Cisco press release, http://newsroom.cisco.com/dlls/2011/prod_060111.html (accessed 15 June 2011).

9   Forrester Research, Inc., "U.S. Interactive Marketing Forecast, 2009 to 2014".

10   comScore, 2010 U.S. Digital Year in Review, 7 February 2011 and 2010 Data Passport, December 2010, http://www.comscore.com/Press_Events/Presentations_ Whitepapers (accessed 15 June 2011).

Social media crosses the generational divide.

Social networking no longer belongs to the special cachet of college students and teens looking to pass the time and share photos. The demographics of users can be quite surprising and of particular importance to political campaigns looking to target certain voter groups. Older voters are going online in greater numbers than ever before. Among Internet users ages 50 and older, the use of social networking doubled from 22 percent to 42 percent in 2010. In 2008, the average age of a user of online social networks was 33. In 2010, it rose to 38, with over half of all adult users of social media over the age of 35.[11]

Older users are now becoming social media's most enthusiastic fans, embracing new technologies and platforms to share links, photos, videos and news updates with their friends, colleagues, and family members. The older set has been traditionally slow to embrace the technology—but all this is now changing. Adults ages 65 and older, followed by those ages 50 to 64, are the fastest growing group of social networking site users, according to the Pew Research Center. [12]

Baby-boomers and seniors are one of the most active demographics on social networking sites. While young adult Internet users dominate on social networking sites, the most robust *growth* came from baby boomers and seniors: 88 percent growth among those ages 50-64 and 100 percent among those 65 and older. [13]

---

11   "Social Networking Sites and Our Lives", 16 June 2011, Pew Internet and American Life Project, http://pewInternet.org/Reports/2011/Technology-and-social-networks/Summary.aspx (accessed 15 June 2011).

12   "Seniors Surge on Social Networking", 15 December 2010, Pew Center Internet and American Life Project, http://www.pewInternet.org/Media-Mentions/2010/Seniors-surge-on-social-networks.aspx (accessed 15 June 2011).

13   "Older Adults and Social Media", 27 August 2010, Pew Center Internet and American Life Project, http://pewresearch.org/pubs/1711/older-adults-social-networking-facebook-twitter (accessed 15 June 2011).

Social networking use continues to grow among older users

The percentage of adult internet users who use social networking sites in each age group

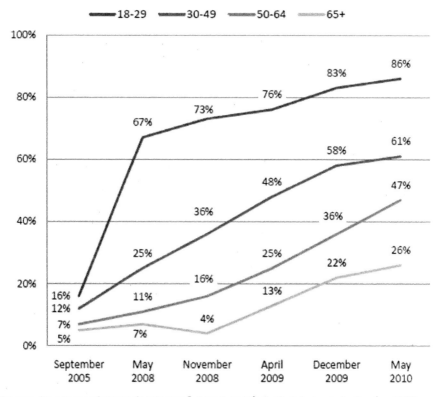

Source: Pew Research Center's Internet & American Life Project Surveys, September 2005 - May, 2010. All surveys are of adults 18 and older.

Social media was originally designed to connect people but now it's being used to share information and to amplify political causes.

People turn to social networking to plan events, mobilize meetings and groups, draw attention to a cause and raise awareness, track down contacts and colleagues, and to cultivate authority— all useful actions for any serious political campaign. Alan Rosenblatt, associate director of online advocacy at the Center for American Progress Action Fund, said that people turn to social networks and social media outlets where they can find recommendations and information from trusted friends. "Given the opportunity to interact with people rather than institutions, people are looking to connect with people they can trust."[14]

People are also increasingly turning to social media for political information. In a Pew study released in March 2011, researchers found that more than half of Internet users (53 percent) went online to engage in campaign-related activities, such as viewing a political video, checking a political claim, or sharing and discussing relevant issues regarding a campaign.[15] In fact, video viewership leading up to the November 2010 mid-term elections rose to 31 percent among adult Internet users, nearly doubling from 2006.

Increasing numbers of Internet users are online participating in activities related to political campaign 'fact-checking'. While the main source of information on campaign news for adults remains television, an increasing number of people (24 percent in 2010) are turning to the Internet for information— more than tripling from the 7 percent in 2002.

Who are these online political users? They are 54 percent of the population, more than half of adults ages 50-64, 61 percent of adults ages 30-49, and nearly 70 percent of young adults (ages 18-29). They tend to be wealthier (77 percent among adults making $75,000 or more) and more educated (3 quarters of post-college grads). Surprisingly, 69 percent of Republicans go online, compared to 56 percent of Democrats— debunking the myth that social media is dominated by the Left.

---

14 "Internet Users Turned to Social Networks in Elections, Survey Finds", 17 March 2011, The New York Times, http://mediadecoder.blogs.nytimes.com/2011/03/17/Internet-users-turned-to-social-networks-in-elections-survey-finds/?ref=technology (accessed 15 June 2011).

15 "The Internet and Campaign 2010", 17 March 2010, Pew Research Center's Internet and American Life Project, http://pewInternet.org/Reports/2011/The-Internet-and-Campaign-2010/Summary.aspx (accessed 15 June 2011).

Online political users

% within each group who are online political users (based on all adults)

All adults	54%
Gender	
Men	56
Women	52
Age	
18-29	67
30-49	61
50-64	53
65+	26
Race/Ethnicity	
White, non-Hispanic	57
Black, non-Hispanic	45
Hispanic	39
Household Income	
Less than $30,000	36
$30,000-$49,999	60
$50,000-$74,999	66
$75,000+	77
Education level	
Some high school	17
High school grad	43
Some college	65
College+	76
Congressional vote	
Republican voters	69
Democratic voters	56
Non-voters	42
Attitude towards Tea Party	
Agree	70
Disagree	66
No opinion	52
Have not heard of	30

Source: The Pew Research Center's Internet & American Life Project, November 3-24, 2010 Post-Election Tracking Survey. N=2,257 national adults ages 18 and older, including 755 cell phone interviews. Interviews were conducted in English and Spanish.

Americans are also using a variety of social media activities to find out what is happening in their communities— including social, economic and political issues.[16] Increasingly, Internet tools are supplanting face-to-face encounters and phone calls. In a 2009 poll, more than one-fifth of all adults signed up to receive alerts on local and community issues (related to school events, crime, social issues, and traffic) via e-mail, text alert, or through a social media account. 20 percent of adults employed digital tools to 'talk' to their neighbors and keep updated on community issues.

Moreover, 11 percent were scouring blogs for information and 6 percent were checking a social networking site or following feeds on Twitter for information. Urbanites tend to gravitate more to blogs. Of those, 17 percent of wired residents in urban areas check community blogs for information, compared to only 11 percent of rural citizens.[17] Among those already on social networks for other reasons, the Pew study showed that 8 percent joined a specialized group focused on a community issue with social media users between the ages of 18 and 49 more likely to join a group than seniors.

Minorities are also using digital technologies and social media platforms to find out what's happening in their communities.[18] African-Americans with access to the web utilize community blogs (18 percent) more than whites (14 percent) and Latinos (13 percent).

---

16   "How Americans Learn About Community Issues", 9 June 2010, Pew Center Internet and American Life Project, http://www.pewInternet.org/Reports/2010/Neighbors-Online/Part-1.aspx (accessed 15 June 2011).

17   "How Americans Learn About Community Issues", 9 June 2010, Pew Center Internet and American Life Project, http://www.pewInternet.org/Reports/2010/Neighbors-Online/Part-1.aspx (accessed 15 June 2011).

18   "How Americans Learn About Community Issues", 9 June 2010, Pew Center Internet and American Life Project, http://www.pewInternet.org/Reports/2010/Neighbors-Online/Part-1.aspx (accessed 15 June 2011).

These studies on information-seeking online underscore the important role that social networks like Facebook and Twitter, as well as technology overall, are likely to play in the upcoming 2012 presidential campaign. Aaron Smith, a senior researcher at the Pew Research Center says, "As more people live more of their lives in the social web, it becomes an important space for them to share their views and interpret what is going on in the world around them." If political campaigns don't have a social media presence, they may lose out.

Candidates around the world have seen the need for digital media and social networking tools as a way to communicate directly with voters in the spaces where they work and play online. With the broader migration among the public toward the digital world taking place, using social media in political campaigns will become more and more necessary.

Mitt Romney's online director, Zac Moffat, has said, "You have to take your message to the places where people are consuming content and spending their time. We have to recognize that people have choices and you have to reach them where they are, and on their terms."[19] According to Laura O'Shaughnessy, general manager at SocialCode, "If the 2008 campaign proved one thing, it's that social media works when it comes to reaching voters who are researching issues online, reading blogs, and debating issues with friends on Facebook."[20]

Social media gives wings to fundraising efforts. In terms of fundraising, Obama was able to raise a steady stream of donations from people donating small amounts and donating frequently. During the campaign,

---

19   "2012 Presidential Candidates 'Friend' Social Media", 17 April 2011, http://www. boston.com/news/local/massachusetts/articles/2011/04/17/2012_presidential_candidates_friend_social_media/ (accessed 15 June 2011).

20   "Facebook is good for research as well as advertising for politicians, study says", 13 June 2011, TechJournal South, http://www.techjournalsouth.com/2011/06/facebook-is-good-for-research-as-well-as-advertising-for-politicians-study-says/ (accessed 15 June 2011).

the average online donation solicited through social media channels was $80. Most online donors gave more than once. In total, Obama raised more than half a billion dollars from over 3 million donors with 6.5 million online donations.[21] The pitch for support made through social media channels resonated with millions of people.

Social media helps influence voters. The Pew Research Center found that 64 percent of online adults think the Internet makes it easier or a lot easier to connect with others who share their views, making social networking an ideal gateway for people to become involved in political activities and issues.[22] Overall, 22 percent of online political users who cast a vote in elections admitted being influenced by online materials and information during the 2010 mid-term elections. 42 percent saw and read online material that swayed their vote one way or another.

As social media becomes another outlet for news, social media galvanizes your base. In the 2008 Presidential election, Republicans and Democrats using the Internet were more likely to get their political news from sites that shared their point of view. The trend continues. In the 2010 mid-term elections, 34 percent of online political users procured news and updates from sites that shared their political views. Corroborating findings in the 2008, both conservatives and liberals in 2010 typically obtained political news from sources sharing their same viewpoints on issues. Campaigns can use this tendency to 'go with the flock' to energize its base through social media.

---

21   "How Obama Won Using Digital and Social Media", http://www.slideshare.net/james.burnes/how-obama-won-using-digital-and-social-media-presentation (accessed 15 June 2011).

22   "The Internet and Campaign 2010", 17 March 2010, Pew Center Internet and American Life Project, http://pewInternet.org/Reports/2011/The-Internet-and-Campaign-2010/Summary.aspx (accessed 15 June 2011).

Social media can be used to sway independents and those who are unsure.

The same study found that people also see the Internet as a place to find information they couldn't find elsewhere. 61 percent of online adults agreed that the Internet provides a *wider* range of political views than traditional news media.[23]

Even now in preparing for the 2012 face-off, Obama kicked off his re-election campaign with this message, which resonated over e-mail and on Facebook to his Democratic supporters. "We'll start by doing something unprecedented: coordinating millions of one-on-one conversations between supporters across every single state, reconnecting old friends, inspiring new ones to join the cause, and readying ourselves for next year's fight," Obama said. "This will be my final campaign, at least as a candidate. But the cause of making a lasting difference for our families, our communities, and our country has never been about one person. And it will succeed only if we work together."[24]

Visitors to his website, BarackObama.com, now find a campaign gearing up to go for the 2012 fight. First, visitors see a splash page that poses a blunt, catchy question, "Are You In?" Facebook fans can announce to their social networks that they are throwing their support behind Obama by entering their e-mail and publicizing on their Facebook wall, "I'm in". From there, BarackObama.com greeted visitors with a 2-minute video featuring— not him giving a speech— but *supporters* reaffirming their support of the President.

---

23   "The Internet and Campaign 2010", 17 March 2010, Pew Center Internet and American Life Project, http://pewInternet.org/Reports/2011/The-Internet-and-Campaign-2010/Summary.aspx (accessed 15 June 2011).

24   "Are You In?: Obama Pitches 2012 as a Group Project", 4 April 2011, TechPresident, http://techpresident.com/short-post/are-you-obama-pitches-2012-group-project (accessed 15 June 2011).

In interviews, people shared their reasons for continuing their support and why Obama should win the re-election. The page with the video included a feature where you could share the clip and invite friends in your social network to join the campaign. The page is pared down at the moment, mostly focused on getting people involved and to commit that they are "in"— committed to volunteer, form a group, give a donation, pass the message, and most of all— to win. The message is clearly one of collaboration, echoing the grassroots tone of his 2008 campaign, and marking a political strategy that is decidedly social at heart.

Chapter 3

Social Elections Launching Winning Campaigns

IN THE old way of running a political campaign, most contenders and candidates took their message to the TV sets of their constituents, spending money on expensive TV ad campaigns, which afforded at most, 30-second to one-minute time slots. With a blink of an eye, passive prospective voters could see a campaign's message, and got very little follow-up or engagement. As a result, viewers were numbingly bombarded with commercials. Another way politicians tried to reach voters was through physical signage— placards and billboards posted around towns, ads in newspapers and magazines and other print media. These traditional campaign strategies demanded big, bloated advertising budgets.

In today's political campaigns, supporters interact with political campaigns in decidedly different ways. Much of these changes are driven by advances in technology related to social media and social networking in digital spaces— new platforms, tools, devices that make it easier but also more complicated to reach and engage potential voters. "The tools changed between 2004 and 2008. Barack Obama won every single caucus state that matters, and he did it because of those tools, because he was able to move thousands of people to organize," says Joe Trippi, a political consultant and former campaign organizer for Howard Dean.[25]

Today, digital technologies and social media have made the same mobilization much easier and more cost-effective. In the past, an army of organized volunteers and paid staffers would have been needed to mount such mass mobilization at the local level that was seen in the Obama campaign in 2008. For example, political campaigns are now increasingly savvy about adapting mobile computing tools, which were initially designed for consumer marketing, for voter mobilization and fundraising. According to Brett Broesder, a marketing executive at Hill & Knowlton, "Social media, such as Facebook, is used by a vast array of voters in multiple demographics, and remains an inexpensive venue to connect with people directly." This makes it a very valuable asset for cash-strapped campaigns.[26]

---

25 "Obama Facebook Town Hall Meeting with Mark Zuckerberg", 5 April 2011, http://dailycaller.com/2011/04/05/obama-to-hold-facebook-town-hall-meeting-with-mark-zuckerberg/ (accessed 29 June 2011).

26 "New Social media and the 2012 Election: Waaaaay Beyond Facebook 2008", Christian Science Monitor, 20 April 2011, http://www.csmonitor.com/USA/Society/2011/0420/New-social-media-and-the-2012-election-Waaaaay-beyond-Facebook-2008/%28page%29/2 (accessed 15 June 2011).

With the new technology available, imagine this scenario, which is becoming more and more commonplace:

At a political rally you attend (which was announced via text message alerts), you check-in on Foursquare or through Facebook using your smartphone or tablet that optically scans a QR bar code on a poster at the door. The QR bar code enables you to make a digital connection with the campaign and to let your social network know that you're attending a rally at this particular location. With check-ins, organizers can give you digital badges or other rewards, such as freebies, for participation. In addition, scanning the QR bar code downloads an event agenda or program, which may be a file or an interactive app. As you launch the document or app, you are automatically logged by the event organizers who post your participation on Facebook or on the campaign website. In addition, your e-mail address, Twitter handle or other social networking identities can be recorded by the campaign into a database for future correspondence and fundraising appeals. With a text message or e-mail, you can donate money with a few clicks.

Getting into the Social Media Mindset

What's Your Social Media Strategy?

The stratospheric growth of social media isn't hyperbole anymore or a trend that will fade away— it's an entrenched part of the political landscape— with millions of people frequenting social media websites. For political campaigns to benefit from this virtual public square, they must embrace it fully. Social media connects you with voters and constituents in an interconnected hub that is both informal and one-on-one. In many ways, social media is anti-campaigning; it lets you build a reputation and brand and attracts a core community of supporters, as well as reaches out to potential supporters in a loose, unstructured way. With social media, campaigns are able to reach out in more personal and direct ways than is possible using traditional campaign tactics.

Commenting on the impact of social media, Amazon.com CEO Jeff Bezos once said, "If you make customers unhappy in the physical world, they might tell six people, their closest friends. If you make customers unhappy on the Internet, they can each tell 6,000 people." The power of social media is in its ability to reach a wider number of people. Every revolutionary presidential campaign teetered on how the candidate reached its audience. Franklin D. Roosevelt was a charismatic leader on the radio, using his stentorian voice and the cadence of speech to mesmerize and inspire people over the airwaves. John F. Kennedy is known for being a sterling candidate on television, looking fresh and charismatic next to a tired-looking Richard Nixon in the first-ever televised debates. Howard Dean introduced the power of organization and fundraising over the web. And Barack Obama was the first politician to really understand how to create a political brand through social media. In the age of Facebook and Twitter, Obama and his campaign understand the power of decentralized, grassroots campaigning through digital networks, creating a sense of connection and engagement that propelled people to self-organize.

Make sure your campaign team understands the core and nature of social media and all that it encompasses.

The team needs to understand not only the essential tools and how they work, but also how to engage people through those digital tools and the importance of social media in electoral politics and campaigns of all stripes.

Social media has democratized the democratic process one step further—and makes it possible for the little guy to have an impact. The first breakthrough in formulating a strategy is to *understand* the nuances of the change. Andrew Rasiej, the founder of the Personal Democracy Forum, has predicted that "any politician who fails to recognize that we are in a post-party era with a new political ecology in which connecting like minds and forming a movement is so much easier will not be around long." [27]

Undergo a frank social media assessment test with your campaign team.

Before whisking off to create your Facebook fan page and Twitter account, here are several questions to consider carefully:

1. What are your campaign's social media goals? Getting the candidate into the spotlight? Firing up the political base?

2. Do your campaign organizers know how to use the basic social media tools available? If not, are there plans to hire digital media specialists to train your staff?

---

27 "The Media Equation: How Obama Tapped into Social Networks' Power", 9 November 2008, The New York Times http://www.nytimes.com/2008/11/10/business/media/10carr.html (accessed 20 June 2011).

3. Who will be on your digital media team? Will they have direct access to your campaign manager? To the candidate?

4. Do you have metrics in place to know which social media channels are the most effective for your campaign? Is your organization agile enough to make changes on the fly?

5. What infrastructure is already in place to start the social media campaign? Do we start with a website or a Facebook page?

Use a stepped approach to launch your campaign— and do it better than your opponent.

While many point to Obama's 2008 campaign as revolutionary in its use of social media, the truth is that it wasn't doing what hadn't been done before. In fact, his opponents were using the same tools and services. The difference was that he did it better— incrementally better— than the competition. Strategic decisions were made down to the nitty-gritty details for every e-mail and for the look-and-feel of the website. The bottom line was— compared to his challengers, he better understood the power of community in these new channels.

Edelman, in their report, *The Social Pulpit*, advocates using a stepped approach to launching your social media strategy:[28]

---

28   "The Social Pulpit: Barack Obama's Social Media Toolkit", January 2009, Edelman Digital Public Affairs, http://www.edelman.com/image/insights/content/social%20pulpit%20-%20barack%20obamas%20social%20media%20toolkit%201.09.pdf (accessed 20 June 2011).

Advocate — Recruit others to donate / Host an event / Create a group

Social — Post pictures/videos / Write a blog post / Join a group

Personal — Create a profile / Post a comment / Make a donation / Sign-up for e-mail/SMS / Friend on social networks

Structured sequencing in getting your social media campaign off the ground ensures that you have covered your bases:

1. **Establish your core digital presence.**
   Invest in producing a clean and attractive website and campaign profiles on all the basic social media platforms.

2. **Focus on fresh and informative content.**
   Feed your social media platforms a steady diet of crowdsourced (created by your supporters) and original blogs, videos, pictures, and other material.

3. **Network and embrace community.**
   Maintain a dialogue with your supporters on the various social media platforms. Ask your super supporters to write and share stories about their campaign experience on your sites and others. Contact political news heavyweights in the blogosphere.

Ensure that you have the resources to invest time and attention to your social media strategies.

Remember, a social media program isn't icing on the cake anymore— it is a core, *substantive* part of your campaign. Invest time into creating a sensible plan and make sure your team, from the rank-and-file staffers to the candidate, has a keen understanding of what it takes. Most of all, invest in the quality of engagement in the various social media platforms because that will determine the quality of the community you are building.

Track key metrics to test your campaign's performance on social media platforms.

Many social media platforms, such as Facebook, offer built-in metrics to track your campaign's impact on the blogosphere, Twitterverse, and the web at large. Campaign website metrics to watch include visits from social media sites, leads, inquiries, and newsletter or e-mail signups from social media sites. Facebook issues a 'Facebook Insights' page that enables you to track interaction from your supporters (how many fans have 'Liked' a post); and the number of supporters your page has attracted (the size of your Facebook social network and new members added in the past week). In addition, make use of Google alerts, Tweetmeme, and other social media 'listening' tools to track your social media footprint.

Chapter 4

The Basics: Must-Have Platforms For Electoral Success

CAMPAIGNERS SHOULD make use of several core social networking sites as their campaign 'social media dashboards' from which they can control their messaging and image, as well as mobilize support and coordinate fundraising efforts. As campaign expert Zac Moffat has said, while every campaign may have a physical headquarters somewhere— it also needs 'digital embassies' across the web.

The basic platforms and tools for launching a social media-friendly political campaign include:

- **Website**
- **Blog**
- **Facebook**
- **Twitter**
- **Google/YouTube**
- **LinkedIn**

Websites: Your Campaign's Digital Focal Point

A good campaign needs a good website. Gone are the days of politicians merely worrying about how a television interview went or how they were perceived on a radio campaign. Now, politicians must consider things like Facebook, Twitter, Flickr and— most importantly— the campaign website.

Why it Matters

If a political campaign is to be effective, it must reach a voter, clearly, and consistently, at every level of interaction. Although television, radio, newspapers, magazines, Twitter, Facebook, Flickr, and others, shape a voter's perception of who a candidate is, none of these are quite so 'real' as the politician's website. As most voters will never get to meet a politician face-to-face, a well-designed website is crucial to a successful campaign. In many ways, a website essentially becomes the candidate; the experience that a voter has with a politician's website— good or bad— is often the most significant interaction he or she will have with that politician.

And, while Twitter, Facebook, and the like all have their merits, none of them have the capability of employing the intricate design, copy, and 'feel' of a candidate's website. Thus, a well-designed website can do a great deal of good for a political campaign, while a poorly designed website can lose a voter within seconds.

Think of a political campaign's website as the equivalent of your social media headquarters, the centralized location for reaching your voters and supporters. MyBarackObama.com (MyBO) functioned as the starting platform from which to extend the organization. As individual networks sprouted on Facebook and MySpace, the website served as a means to coordinate and unify the message of each extended and independently functioning 'digital embassy'. It allowed the 2008 Obama campaign to organize and amplify the growth and reach of its core site without degrading its grassroots momentum.

Echoes of the Obama campaign can be found in the grassroots mobilization of Howard Dean's campaign in 2004. Dean's campaign was one of the earliest attempts at using the web to fundraise and to generate political buzz and organize voter outreach— though in the end, Dean was unable to convert his online infrastructure into votes on the ground. By 2008, Obama's campaign strategists decided to focus on how to generate the same level of grassroots excitement into votes. They did this through a well-honed social media strategy at which the MyBO website was at the heart.

According to Quantcast.com, here's how three campaign sites rated in the 2008 Presidential election, with Obama clearly leading by a wide margin.

Barack Obama 2008[29]

Estimated Monthly Uniques (US) = 199,369

Stickiness: 37% of visitors are regulars; 20% are addicts

Subdomains: 12

Keyword Affinity: www.obama.com, barak obama, obama

Quantcast says: "Barackobama.com is a top 10,000 site that reaches over 199K U.S. monthly uniques. The site is popular among a primarily older, more educated, primarily female, more African American following."

---

29   Quantcast, http://www.quantcast.com/barackobama.com (accessed 20 June 2011).

Hilary Clinton 2008[30]

Estimated Monthly Uniques (US) = 139,649

Stickiness: 42% of visitors are regulars; 14% are addicts

Subdomains: 5

Keyword Affinity: clinton campaign, hillary for president, clinton for president

Quantcast says: "This site reaches over 139K U.S. monthly uniques. The site caters to a more educated, primarily older, slightly female slanted audience."

Ron Paul 2008[31]

Estimated Monthly Uniques (US) = 102,053

Stickiness: 55% of visitors are regulars; 6% are addicts

Subdomains: 2

Keyword Affinity: ron paul for president, ron paul

Quantcast says: "This site reaches over 102K U.S. monthly uniques. The site attracts a somewhat male, primarily older following."

---

30   Quantcast, http://www.quantcast.com/hillaryclinton.com (accessed 20 June 2011).

31   Quantcast, http://www.quantcast.com/ronpaul2008.com (accessed 20 June 2011).

Strategies for Optimal Use

1. Create a sense of community.

Websites should foster a supportive online atmosphere that gives supporters the resources to mount their own grassroots drives and campaigns. They should offer tutorials on using the online tools, as well as primers and booklets for download that can help organizers plan events, such as fundraising and voter outreach.

As your local groups use your online tools, make sure you thank them and provide a means for them to exchange tips and advice. In Obama's 2008 Presidential campaign, MyBO members were also treated to weekly conference calls from campaign staff that offered feedback on ideas. It was also a way for local members to report back to headquarters about an event that went smoothly (or not) and get encouragement and advice.

2. Design with usability in mind.

Make sure it's easy for your users to navigate and find the information they need, participate in discussions, and stay updated with the campaign. The MyBO campaign promoted several key functional elements that are worth adopting for your campaign website: a dashboard, profile, action center, fundraising, network, and sidebar.[32]

Dashboard: When MyBO users logged in at the website, the first thing they saw was the dashboard. It served as the user's homepage and gave users an overview of what was happening at MyBO and provided

---

32   Harfoush, Rahaf, 2009, Yes We Did: An Inside Look at How Social Media Built the Obama Brand (Berkeley: New Riders), p. 76.

shortcuts to tools related to event planning and personal fundraising. Keeping these links in prominent positions gave them an easy-access feel.

Profile: In their profiles, users could post photos, create a user name, and indicate a location. The profile asked users to post their answers to two questions: "Why do you support Barack Obama?" and "Are you registered to vote?" Users could customize their profiles accordingly and share their thoughts with a related blog feature.

Action Center: The MyBO campaign made sure to avoid the mistakes of the Howard Dean campaign of 2004, which failed to carry over the online enthusiasm into votes on the ground— by ensuring that supporter sentiments were actionable. On the website's 'Action Center' corner on the front-page, supporters were given several options to channel their enthusiasm into action, including: 1) knock on doors, 2) make calls, 3) volunteer, 4) find events, and 5) login to MyBO. This ensured that every visitor to the site could immediately see something tangible they could do that would help to achieve the campaign objectives.

Fundraising: Every user who registered with MyBO could set up his or her own fundraising page that included a dynamic image of a thermometer gauge that monitored the progress of money raised to meet a particular goal. As users raised money, the temperature gauge showed the percentage of the goal that had been met so far. Each fundraising page included an embed code and customizable URL that could be added to personal websites and e-mails. Here, fundraising efforts were redirected not to total strangers but to each supporter's own social network. Users weren't encouraged just to make cold calls to fundraise, but to solicit their friends and family. It made the campaign more personal and meaningful for many. People who normally didn't give to campaigns were now donating money because they were donating on behalf of someone they knew. MyBO supporters who managed their fundraising pages were more committed to raising money because it constituted a personal goal. During the campaign, MyBO supporters with fundraising pages collected more than $35 million in donations.[33]

Network: MyBO made it easy for users to find and interact with other supporters. Messages could be exchanged on the site similar to intra-office e-mail. Contacts from personal e-mails accounts could be exported and uploaded to the site, which encouraged users to send invitations to their friends, family, and wider social networks to join.

Sidebar: When users logged on to MyBO a floating sidebar was always visible even if the user navigated from the dashboard to different pages of the website. This made it easy to access all the functionality with ease and to navigate to key features, such as the message inbox, community information (user groups, friends, neighborhood), action center, fundraising pages, blog, and resource center.

3. Create a consistent typographic palette, color palette, and overall 'look'.

The MyBO campaign wanted something versatile— that could be both simple but elegant, bold but versatile. The campaign took their inspiration for typeface from *GQ* magazine's use of Gotham font, which in turn was based on the letters used by the Port Authority Terminal in New York City. It was the everyday person's font.

Consistent design is important because it reflects the campaign's identity. When potential voters visit a website they want to be greeted by familiar design elements. Many campaigns make the mistake of using flashier elements to garner attention. Instead, focus on the details and stay true to the brand.

---

33 Harfoush, Rahaf, 2009, Yes We Did: An Inside Look at How Social Media Built the Obama Brand (Berkeley: New Riders), p. 76.

4. Design the website architecture to be flexible to allow for changes.

It will take time to create something that isn't too dense with information and busy. Many campaign sites try to pack too much information in a space right away.

Example 1

The MyBO campaign for Barack Obama's 2008 Presidential bid saw its website evolve. The MyBO Campaign expanded its website in three major iterations:[34]

First version: The MyBO campaign used a clean, effortless design with elements placed in a simple, grid layout.

---

34   Images sourced from http://www.bivingsreport.com/2008/the-evolution-of-barack-obamas-campaign-website/ (accessed 20 June 2011).

Second version: The minimalist design of the first version of the site transformed into a much more cluttered layout with this second version. Banner ads were squeezed onto the page in order to pack enough information for the reader, but it soon became an eye sore. Instead of just six elements on the page, the site bloated itself with 11 elements on the same real estate space.

CAUTION: As campaigns grow and expand, there is a tendency for teams to constantly add more information and links, which risks overrunning the page and diluting the impact on readers.

Final version: In terms of design, this third version of the MyBO website was where the campaign hit its stride. Aligned with its message of hope, the site took on a strong design aesthetic with its high-gloss images and deep, rich colors with subtle shadings. It looked vibrant on LCD monitors. Load time, however, was slower for some viewers because of the design elements.

Technically, the Obama campaign used a top layer story area using Flash or javascript/Ajax, which enabled the ability to rotate different headlines without the clutter that plagued the second version. Today, this appears to be a standard design element for many organizations that use different headlines.

The new design was clean and offered visitors clear choices, making it easy to navigate. Two main columns dominated, blog-inspired in style and encouraged readers to scroll.

MyBO later won recognition at the Cannes Lion International Advertising Awards in 2009— snatching the Titanium grand prix and the Integrated Lions category, an honor that goes to a campaign that is "provocative, challenges assumptions and points to a new direction".[35]

---

35   Cannes Lions International Festival of Creativity, http://www.canneslions.com/ (accessed 20 June 2011).

Example 2

Change.gov

When Obama won the 2008 Presidential Election, the campaign put together Change.gov, which carried on much of the message and design elements of the campaign site. It featured a top-level link, which outlined Obama's policies, as well as a blog and the latest announcements and information for the press. On election night, the first blog post covered Obama's victory speech. Change.gov was intended to be a simple transition of the campaign web site and to carry on the online momentum of supporters, keeping them engaged and plugged-in post-victory.

Example 3

Obama's 2012 website

Reflecting the principle of flexibility, Obama's 2012 website is a lot more minimalist than before which, according to an entry on the site's new blog, is because they wish to "start small— online and off— and develop something new in the coming weeks and months." According to a blog on the website, "The idea is to improve upon what's worked for the past four years, scrap what hasn't, and build a campaign that reflects the thoughts and experiences of the supporters who've powered this movement." The blog encourages users to comment and give feedback on the campaign and on Obama's policies. It also fuses communications on numerous sites: a blog entry is automatically tweeted on Obama's Twitter feed, for instance.

Example 4

Prime Minister Benjamin Netanyahu

Many websites have followed the stylistic conventions of Barack Obama's 2008 website. None more illustrative than the website of Israel's Prime Minister Benjamin Netanyahu. Here, the functionality and aesthetic was completely taken out of the MyBO playbook— including the two-column placement, banner style, and color scheme.

5. Harness the power of the redirect.

When creating links to your site, keep in mind that you want the web server to redirect users to land on a central address. For example, a user that clicks on the link, "barackobama.com" will automatically be delivered to a central web page at http://www.barackobama.com/index. php. The reason the redirect is a powerful Search Engine Optimization technique is that it concentrates the activity to one page, which works to build the ranking of that page on search engines.

If your site does not use redirects, the power of page ranking in searches is diluted, fragmenting where the user goes and splitting up the number of visits that search engines tally. This is known as "splitting pagerank". The Hilary Clinton and Ron Paul websites did not use redirects as effectively, which resulted in their sites appearing as active at the root domain level *and* the www subdomain level— in effect, splitting the page ranks for search engines.

6. Make use of strategic subdomains.

Subdomains are sites that fall under a particular master domain or central website, often with different content and focus than the main website. But because search engines see subdomains as different sites, they do not add to the page rankings of your parent site— unless you have a redirect (see point 5). You may want to consider creating a sub-directory structure, instead, unless you have a substantial amount of specialized content that needs to be separated in subdomains.

When using subdomains, use them strategically. You should only use subdomains when you have enough content to justify the use of it (and don't forget redirects). For Obama's 2008 campaign site, Quantcast counted 12 subdomains. Hilary Clinton's site listed 5 subdomains and the Ron Paul site had only 2. Barack Obama's subdomains included action, donate, story, Iowa, answercenter, signup, women, faith, students, Illinois, Nevada, my, NH (for New Hampshire), SC (for South Carolina) and others.

How many subdomains your website has will impact the search results in Google, Bing, and other search engines. For example, if you searched under the term "BarackObama" on Google, the search results show that the "Obama for America 2012" re-election campaign website comes up first; in effect, it has the highest number of subdomains, followed by the WhiteHouse.gov site.

7. Engage users at all levels, and encourage them to provide stories, opinions, and engage in dialogue.

Many have called 2006 a watershed year for social media, when the digital space was dubbed Web 2.0. Web 2.0 was an evolution of user interaction on the Internet. Users were no longer passive receptacles of information, but were now active contributors, turning the web into a place where digital content was shared. In the social media-driven online political space today, this means that supporters are uploading content and materials and sharing them with supporters.

Example 1

Obama 2008 Campaign's continuum of incentives and support

To keep its members and supporters engaged and motivated, the Obama 2008 Campaign team made sure they provided incentives for people to take certain actions. They first came up with an incentive scheme based on points that were earned by MyBO members: 15 points for hosted events, 15 points for a donation made on the personal fundraising page, 10 points for every door knocked on using an online canvassing tool, 5 points for phone calls made using an online tool, 3 points for a group joined, and 3 points for each blog post. Ironically, mobilization in the offline world was more valued because it was the leap from online to offline that was viewed as catalyzing votes.

Cumulative scores were calculated and displayed on the user's profile with a rank that indicated where you stood relative to other members. Users could immediately see what impact their participation was having in the context of the campaign, creating more incentives to engage more.

Later, the point system evolved to an indexed system. The index created a more transparent way to show how users had engaged; that is, how many people they called, how many events they attended. The index evaluated the activity level on a 1-10 scale, with 10 being the most active. The index only took into account recent activity, which meant that users had an even greater incentive to maintain participation levels, ensuring a steady activity level and buzz among users.

As ratings increased, users could earn special privileges like gaining access to training videos. Super users were spotted by campaign leaders and tapped to assume more visible roles, such as lead a phonebank campaign or mobilize local groups. The index system allowed campaign organizers to identify and recruit these dedicated supporters.

Example 2

Dilma Rousseff for President in Brazil: Engaging users

Brazilian politics were still new to grassroots campaigning, making online mobilization difficult. Dilma Rousseff was in a strong position to win, but she had little name recognition and was most known to voters by her association with the popular incumbent president, Lula.

Dilma's campaign hired Blue State Digital (the same company that assisted in Barack Obama's 2008 campaign site) to design their campaign website with the goal of improving online interaction with potential voters. The site brought this interactivity to a new level by allowing ideas, stories, and thoughts to be shared through the site's forums.

The website was also savvy in its use of these voter stories to add emotional resonance to the content of the site and to create a humanistic backdrop to the social and economic issues highlighted by Dilma's campaign. Engagement with voters was available via Twitter and various forums, which could be accessed directly from the site. The website was also carefully coordinated with an e-mail campaign that targeted specific active supporters, updated them on travel schedules and engagements, and announced offline events.

Blogs: A More Personalized Campaign Voice

Depending on how they are used, blogs and public forums can enhance political campaigns and your social media presence in effective ways. Most campaigns tend to look at blogs as built-in components of their websites. Blogs provide a ready sounding-board for a campaign to make its voice known. Much more extensive than a Facebook post or your haiku-esque tweet, blogs can be time-consuming and require a big investment of research and writing. While tweets are high-frequency announcements and thoughts, blogs are less infrequent and can seem like epic pronouncements by comparison. The ideal length of a blog can range from shorter pieces of about 500-700 words to longer features, which can go as high as 1,500 words. Long-form (around 1,000 words) is preferable. Blogs require more discursive thought and research, but can leave visitors more satisfied than your typical tweet or Facebook post.

Why it Matters

Most content on campaign websites can feel stilted, giving visitors little reason to visit unless they need routine and basic information about a campaign. They read like brochures or press releases and provide official bios on candidates.

Blogs provide an opportunity for campaigns to add a more personal dimension to a site. Blogs are a great opportunity to reach out to potential voters and supporters on fundraising and volunteering opportunities using a personal angle. The flexibility on length and form allows campaigns to offer a more narrative-driven content. While political Facebook posts and tweets rarely stray from messaging, blogs should read like real, authentic thoughts from the candidate and campaign. They shouldn't sound like a canned speech or an op-ed that's been vetted by lawyers and devoid of emotion and personality. In fact, blogs can be a little bit more digressive in style and topics.

Strategies for Optimal Use

1. Engage readers in new and unique ways.

Visitors checking your campaign blog are usually looking for extra information on a candidate beyond credentials and the usual campaign sound bites. In fact, leave the posting of campaign news and related press releases out of your blog. Campaign blogs can have the most impact when they are truly personal and stripped down of the 'campaign language'. Share insights and opinions— because it's these personal takes that will make readers flock to your site.

While the overall goal of the blog is to add another social media platform from which to engage the public and should align with the overall stance of the campaign, it can also be used to boost campaigns in a different way— by veering outside the orbit of the usual gamut of topics. Loosen the grip on messaging carefully, but try engaging readers by appealing to their non-political interests.

The Obama 2008 presidential campaign offered an opportunity for its MyBO members to post blogs about their experiences involving the campaign. Popular blogs expressed how Barack Obama's previous work or speeches touched their lives. One supporter blogged about how a speech Obama made at a Citizens United for Research in Epilepsy (CURE) event touched her and gave her comfort in light of the fact that her daughter died from the medical condition. The blog connected some aspect of Barack Obama to her personal plight.

Maria later took her enthusiasm and marshaled other supporters and raised money by launching her own campaign on her MyBO page. It involved collecting recipes from other fellow Obama supporters and compiling it into an online cookbook. The stories were intertwined with recipes and conveyed a sense of deep community from a shared love of food and passion for the campaign.

2. Establish a regular writing/publishing schedule.

Blogging requires a fair amount of time to be invested in research and writing and cultivating a strong narrative voice. If the campaign doesn't prioritize blogging, it will languish. An inactive blog can mar the perception of a candidate among website visitors.

Is the candidate going to author the blogs? Will key campaign staffers take turns posting? Blogs should be updated fairly frequently to avoid long periods of silence and inactivity. Readership takes time to build and traction depends on keeping current readers coming back and building traffic to your site from frequent blog checks. Blogs should be updated on a fairly regular basis: once or twice a week for long form posts (800 to 1,500 words) and daily for shorter blog articles (400-700 words).

3. Use blogs to provide behind-the-scenes information on events and news items mentioned on Facebook and Twitter.

One way blogs can complement your other content on Facebook and Twitter is to expand on the information presented. Go beyond the usual talking-points and messaging to get readers engaged and emotionally-invested in your campaign. Blogs can function as a place where your visitors can find 'special features'— much like the movie extras on DVDs.

Some ideas for special features for your political blog include:

- **Behind-the-scenes commentary on activity at campaign headquarters.**

- **Discussion on the opponent's views on key issues— and why your strategy is a better way of tackling them.**

- **Profiles of top campaign staffers.**

- **Spotlights on key supporters, volunteers, and extraordinary campaign efforts from real people.**

- **'Straight talk' Q&A sessions with the candidate.**

- **Responses and editorials on current events and news stories.**

- **First-person accounts of town-hall meetings, stump speeches, and phonebanking events.**

- **Special messages from the candidate to supporters.**

- **Guest posts from other politicos endorsing the candidate.**

- **Reactions to news stories, blogs, and editorials that mention your campaign.**

4. Reach out to the blogosphere.

An important component of your blog strategy is blog outreach. Blogs should not exist in a vacuum; otherwise your campaign risks being limited to only reaching its existing base (the 'preaching to the choir' syndrome). The blogosphere is vast and interconnected. To expand your reach outside your core circle of supporters toward potential voters, build a network of guest bloggers in support of your candidate. This ensures that your campaign builds credibility and allies across the political sphere and reaches a bigger audience. Not only should your campaign be blogging on its own site, but it should also volunteer to write guest entries on other popular blog networks, such as *DailyKos* and *RedState*.

Have a few staff members take the time to write comments on political blogs. Commenting gives you another channel to connect with the author of the blog post and its readers. Another by-product of responding to other blogs is that any links or commentary you make are searchable, helping you rack up more 'hits' to your own campaign site.

Follow a few common etiquette rules on commenting on blogs:

- **Be brief:** While you may be tempted to write long, extensive replies on important political topics, readers will appreciate pithy responses. Zone in on what struck a chord with you and resonates with your campaign and stance on relevant issues. Add a link to external pages (preferably your website or blog) where additional information can be provided to readers. Comments sometimes morph into their own standalone blog posts, so see how the conversation goes and what 'material' and insights you can cull from the experience and relate in a blog article. Always refer back to the blog post or specific comment that incited your blog article or comment.

- **Make sure you identify yourself in the comment.** Anonymous comments have no teeth and are dead-ends for readers. Take the time to write measured and thoughtful comments and be sure to include a link to your campaign web site or blog.

- **Stay on topic.** Straying from the conversation can be disruptive and invites blog owners to delete your comment or prompts other readers to jump on your non-sequitor commentary. Make reference to specific points in the article and provide your insights and analysis on the ideas presented.

- **Be forthright but be polite.** No one wants a political blowhard dominating the conversation. Comments are a place to speak your mind, there is always a measured way of making your points known. Keep the strong rhetoric off comments and on your own blog or website.

5. Enable the comment feature on your blogs and add social media plug-ins

Blogs offer the greatest power for a campaign when they are shared and passed around by your supporters, first-time visitors, and even opponents. Make the sharing process easier by adding social plug-ins, which enable your readers to quickly share your blog article on a variety of other social media channels like Facebook, Twitter, LinkedIn.

Encourage your blog readers to post comments. This engages your audience emotionally and stimulates conversations that can build deeper and stronger relationships between your supporters and campaign. While you can delete and police extreme and blatantly offensive comments, avoid the urge to censor and edit commentary— particularly from naysayers and your opponent's fans. Blogs that have a wide range of comments have more clout and credibility than blogs that elicit very little response. Visitors that post comments also build valuable links to your campaign site from external sites, building your rank in search engines like Google and Bing.

Using The Social Networks
Facebook: The World's Number One Social Networking Platform

Facebook's foray into electoral politics has intensified over the years. In 2008, it launched a partnership with the non-partisan 'Voting Information Project'. Together, they created the Polling Place Locator, an application that lets visitors find out where they can vote.

With more than half a billion users, Facebook has become the number one platform where citizens of the world connect, cultivating online identities in personal profile pages, and communicating with family, friends and colleagues by posting articles, comments, likes and dislikes, and indulging common interest with others.

Why it Matters

It would be a political misstep to think of Facebook as only a social networking site for leisure and sharing photos. Facebook has become the juggernaut driving web traffic. In 2010, more than 2.5 million websites integrated with Facebook, including 80 percent of comScore's top 1000 U.S. web sites.[36] Users can now log in directly at numerous websites using their Facebook accounts. On a monthly basis, more than a quarter of a million people access Facebook using Facebook Connect, a one-click sign-in button accessible through various websites. Instead of creating separate accounts, users can use Facebook as their central account. Its 700 million members make it bigger than the size of the U.S. and a digital nation all its own.

---

36   Facebook Press Room/Statistics, http://www.facebook.com/press/info. php?statistics (accessed 20 June 2011).

In a survey conducted by the Pew Research Center over the November 2010 mid-term elections, researchers found that compared to the average online American who engages in social networking, Facebook users were 2.5 times more likely to attend a political rally or meeting, 57 percent more likely to influence someone to vote and 43 percent more likely to vote or express intentions to vote.[37] Compared with non-users, Facebook users were 5.89 times more likely to have attended a meeting, 2.79 times more likely to talk to someone about their vote, and 2.19 times more likely to report voting.

With the right strategies, political campaigns can use Facebook to reach wider audiences and at a deeper and more personal level. Facebook offers the critical mass of information that is highly regarded in political analysis and extremely useful. As more information is shared, more data can be collected. The tiny 'Like' button has become a de facto barometer to predict election results. Facebook also has something else that helps campaigns: the power of peer pressure. We are all more likely to vote for candidates our friends have liked, for example. Campaigns need to develop their candidates as a brand and use Facebook for outreach and validation.

In November 2010 mid-term elections, news analysts were watching the numbers rise for candidates, but they weren't referring to the poll numbers— they were referring to the number of Facebook fans. The number of Facebook fans a candidate had was seen as a leading indicator of the outcome of the race. Pundits talked about who had the most fans on Facebook, building on the perceived popularity of candidates and building clout. If the Facebook fans were right, the Republicans were predicted to trounce the Democrats in the races. The Facebook indicators were accurate.

---

37   "Social Networking Sites and Our Lives", 16 June 2011, Pew Center Internet and American Life Project, http://pewInternet.org/Reports/2011/Technology-and-social-networks/Summary.aspx (accessed 20 June 2011).

On Election Day 2010, Republican candidates beat Democratic opponents by margins that were better than two-to-one, giving the house back to the GOP. Here's how the Facebook numbers looked. Democrats in all the House, Senate, and gubernatorial races had a total of 1,444,992 fans, while the Republican candidates had 3,459,799 Facebook fans.[38] Over 51,000 fans went to independent candidates. Facebook's own metrics of the political scene found that out of an initial snapshot of 98 House races, 74 percent of candidates with the most Facebook fans won their contests.[39] In an initial snapshot of 19 races for the Senate, 81 percent of those candidates with the most Facebook fans won their contests.

Facebook wasn't always a surefire barometer for picking Election Night winners. According to Nancy Scola of *Tech Nation*, in close races the number of Facebook fans opposing candidates had did not accurately predict who won in the voter's booth— amounting to nothing more than a cloudy crystal ball.[40] [41] In the Nevada Senate race between Republican Sharron Angle and Democrat Harry Reid, Reid ultimately claimed victory despite having less support on Facebook than Angle.

Still, even if Facebook isn't a surefire predictor of election wins and losses, it's a solid indicator and it's hard to ignore the impact of

---

38   Numbers cited are according to AllFacebook.com (http://statistics.allfacebook. com/election), a website that tracks 18 million Facebook pages (accessed 20 June 2011).

39   Facebook analysis of the November 2010 elections was listed here: http://www. facebook.com/USpolitics (accessed 20 June 2011).

40   "Facebook's Cloudy Crystal Ball", 3 November 2010, http://www.blogher.com/ frame.php?url=http://techpresident.com/blog-entry/facebooks-cloudy-crystal-ball (accessed 20 June 2011).

41   "Political campaigns embrace social media but can Facebook really predict an election?", http://www.raleighpublicrelations.com/political-campaigns-embrace-social-media-but-can-facebook-really-predict-an-election/ (accessed 20 June 2011).

the social networking site on political outcomes. Facebook is now an inextricable part of every savvy campaign strategy.

Facebook has become center-stage for voters to not only broadcast their political affiliations but to brag about their electoral activities. After voting, Facebook users could click a button that put an "I Voted" banner on their Facebook walls. In the wake of the 2010 Elections, it was estimated that around 12 million people clicked the "I Voted" button— doubling the number of voters on Facebook (5.4 million) in 2008.

Facebook is also a site where people can go and participate directly in electoral activities and campaigns. For the November 2010 elections, Facebook teamed up with news and other traditional media for live town hall events. ABC News and Facebook hosted a town hall at the Walter Cronkite School of Journalism and Mass Communications at Arizona State University for a seven-hour show hosted by ABC News correspondent David Muir, Facebook's Randi Zuckerberg, and Natalie Podgorski of Arizona State University. The show was featured live on a special ABC News/Facebook town hall application, on Facebook.com/ABCNews, and Facebook.com/USpolitics.

According to Nielsen research, the amount of time the average person spends on Facebook is now around 55 minutes per day, which provides more than enough time for any political campaign using Facebook to reach people with ad blasts and through news that spreads organically through members' social networks.[42] The research also showed that the average user clicks 'Like' on nine pieces of content and writes about 25 comments each month. Researchers also found that the average user becomes a fan of two pages each month.

Other Facebook user statistics also demonstrate how effective Facebook can be as a political tool: 48 percent of 18-34 year olds check

---

42   Nielsen, 2010 Media Fact Sheet, http://kenburbary.posterous.com/nielsen-2010-media-fact-sheet (accessed 20 June 2011).

Facebook as soon as they wake up. 48 percent of Americans in the same age bracket get their news solely from Facebook. A million links are shared every 20 minutes.[43] A savvy campaign out to win would do well to position themselves visibly in front of this Facebook demographic.

Strategies for Optimal Use

A successful political campaign depends on effective and organized communication with your voter base. Facebook fan pages make communication much easier. As candidates build a fan base, they also build their contact lists of supporters. Building databases with e-mails takes time and money. But with Facebook fans, campaigns can keep their supporters in the loop simply by posting something on the Facebook wall. Not only does this alert active supporters, but each supporter's network also sees any activity the person has with the campaign fan page. It doesn't take too much political acumen to see that a Facebook fan page has significant potential for candidates.

Creating a Facebook fan page for your campaign is simple; only a personal Facebook account is needed initially, and the owner of the personal account acts as the fan page administrator— which means the administrator has control over his fans, content, and promotion of the page itself. Other admins can be added manually later.

---

43   "Campaigns are Won and Lost on Facebook: Social Networking Now the Most Influential Part of the Campaign Puzzle", 11 May 2011, http://www.ibtimes.com/articles/144250/20110511/campaigns-are-won-and-lost-on-facebook-social-networking-now-the-most-influential-part-of-the-campai.htm (accessed 20 June 2011).

Here are several tips for leveraging Facebook as a political campaign tool:

1. Reconcile your Facebook page and your website; drive activity to one place.

Decide what will be the central digital presence for your political campaign: your website or Facebook page. While campaign websites are still the mainstay of politics, Facebook pages offer an alternative for many looking for supporters. Without the IT resources to develop their own social networking features on websites, the interactivity and built-in infrastructure on Facebook pages makes it a viable alternative for many candidates on small budgets. Facebook pages offer add-on features that can mimic the functionality on websites, such as 'welcome' or splash pages and donation solicitation.

Local and smaller campaigns tend to use their Facebook fan pages as their central digital footprint. In Bay City, Texas, Mark Bricker had about 397 fans for a city with a population of only 18,000 people. Jamey Gay in Danville, Kentucky had 571 fans in a city of only 15,500 people. Mount Airy, Maryland's Wendi Peters had about 223 fans for a tiny town of about 8,700.[44]

If your campaign doesn't have its own web site, make sure you outfit your Facebook page with extras, such as a "Welcome" tab, which serves as a landing page for visitors. Wendi Peters offered visitors a brief outline of her candidacy. Peters also offered a Priorities tab, which laid out point-by-point various campaign promises and statements of action. Small campaigns should use their fan pages and post personal stories of

---

44 "Facebook as a Campaign Tool: A Look at Mayoral Candidates", 28 April 2011, http://www.insidefacebook.com/2010/04/28/facebook-as-a-campaign-tool-a-look-at-mayoral-candidates/ (accessed 20 June 2011).

the candidates as background information and ask to be contacted via Facebook. Channeling traffic through one conduit can be more effective than breaking it up.

Include a "Donation" tab on your Facebook page and try not to be too heavy-handed in asking for money. Engage your fans and post often on issues important to the campaign to attract and retain fans. Keep up the political dialogue. Make sure your username is easy to remember, which will make it easy for voters to find you on the web.

If your campaign opts to maintain both a website and Facebook page, make sure you drive traffic from one site to the other by cross-linking materials and posts. For example, updates on your website should also be listed on Facebook as announcements or wall posts so that they show up on member newsfeeds.

Make sure your fans can share your Facebook page postings. Add Facebook Share and Facebook Connect features to your website for postings and other content there. These Java script-based 'widgets' enable your visitors to share and "like" content, which can be easily promoted to users' social networks.

The approach to the Obama 2008 campaign revolved around putting as much power in the hands of regular people to organize their own communities around the central focal point of MyBO. 800,000 people were registered on the site. The strength of social networking on Facebook was complementary targeting an expansion of the ranks of supporters for the MyBO campaign— and to translate online numbers to campaign relevant outcomes— such as fundraising and voter contact.

2. Establish a 'voice' behind your Facebook campaign.

The administrator and creator of your Facebook page may start out behind the scenes initially, but it's always good to personalize the voice behind your postings and content. As fans start interacting with your campaign, responding to questions, answering other fans questions, and generating a conversation with you and other supporters, it might be a good idea to make the identity of the page's social guru known. Keep this identity to the top echelon of the campaign— either the candidate himself or herself, or a top staffer. Fans like to know they are interacting with people at the top and that the candidates they are supporting are accessible.

3. When you do decide to start your fan page, you need to take the initiative and promote it to grow your fan list.

Promote your Facebook fan page widely. Add a link to your campaign website and make an explicit call to action (e.g. "Join us on Facebook"), and send a message to all your personal friends. This gets the ball rolling and kickstarts your Facebook campaign. Also, promote your page to your entire e-mail list. The larger the fan base, the more it will attract new members because of 'exposure' to wider and wider social networks. Be careful not to spam people to avoid alienating fans. First, make sure the page already has a few interesting tidbits and that your page profile is complete.

Once you reach 25 or more fans, you can customize the Facebook URL. Reserve your name or campaign slogan to make it easier for people to search and find your campaign.

4. Plan strategic updates for supporters and cultivate interaction.

Members will expect to receive messages and updates from the campaign and participate in online discussions through the fan page. Members can also share and upload videos with friends; make sure that you enable this interactivity with fans. Many campaigns make the mistake of restricting content on their site to official, vetted material. Campaign supporters appreciate real, authentic content— from videos to photos— created by other supporters. Using only official material can feel stilted and formal, placing distance between you and your supporters. Campaign fan pages should be places where supporters can engage directly with the campaign and the candidate. Lack of interaction and one-way channels only deter new supporters and turn-off your current base.

Candidates often mistakenly tend to have only a broadcast mentality on Facebook— posting information to fan pages like it were a bulletin board rather than going for real interaction and dialogue. Use your website as the sounding board and make use of your Facebook fan page as a platform to engage supporters. Don't limit your status updates to just asking for support or announcing local events.

Ask questions. Campaigns should use Facebook to reach out to supporters and ask them what *they* think about the issues. Ask for opinions, examples, real-life stories and experiences— all ice breakers to get supporters hooked into a dialogue with you and other supporters.

Monitor comments and postings made by fans for hate message and negative comments. Delete hate messages immediately and respond to criticism in a prompt, professional manner. Rebuttals can quickly escalate into 'screaming matches' over Facebook so be careful about letting these debates continue unabated on your campaign fan page. Keep the conversation going· but don't fan any flames and diffuse any extremist points of view.

5. Determine the right level of buzz and activity.

Little activity on the page can make fans forget you have a presence while too much activity can push away many supporters, prompting them to leave your page. Establish a campaign publishing plan that will ensure that regular, quality commentary and posts are made on the page by campaign staff. Posts should always be relevant and informative, but don't be afraid of the occasional quirky personal post, such as expressions of sentiment (e.g. "We're fired up for the rally at 8pm at the Bridge Community Center")— which humanizes the campaign. Posts should also cover not only direct campaign news, but also related news of importance to the campaign, such as news in other states on similar issues and news about opponents and opposing campaigns.

6. Don't overwhelm your fans with too many bulk messages.

Don't send too many bulk direct messages to fans. Aim for once a month or twice per month at the most— and save these for the really important stuff— like big wins or losses. Avoid calls for fundraising through too many bulk messages. Frequent messages clogging up inboxes can be irritating and fans may react by requesting to be removed from your fan page or ignoring the campaign completely. The biggest reaction to avoid among supporters is indifference, which is the number one reason for failing to visit the ballot box on Election Day.

7. Use Facebook to solicit funds from fans.

While your fans and supporters outside your district or area won't be able to vote for you, they can contribute to your campaign and lend a hand by donating funds to your coffer. In previous years, candidates rarely solicited funds outside their districts because it was too expensive or impractical. But now with Facebook ads, it's easier than ever to fundraise across borders. Congressman Jon Runyan ran Facebook ad campaigns to raise money for his bid for New Jersey's third congressional district seat and later won.

8. Using creative Facebook elements to make your page unique.

Add creative banners on your campaign page to differentiate the layout from other generic fan pages. Unlike Twitter, you can add photos, videos, events, and limited HTML elements (also called FBML, a unique Facebook markup language) to enrich your page and make Facebook more engaging for your supporters.

9. Use Facebook Ads and Facebook Sponsored Stories Ads.

Political campaigns can make use of Facebook's ads, which is another tool that can be easily deployed to drive traffic to your Facebook page. Facebook ads can cover local issues or topics of particular importance to your constituents. Variants of the same ad can be targeted to specific types of supporters. When clicked, the ads go to your Facebook page or you can send users to your campaign website.

Now, you may want to lead supporters from the social network site to your campaign site but you will soon find this to be a poor idea.

The model of having fans 'jump to an external site' has its advantages and disadvantages. Why? Fans often don't like leaving the social networking site. They are on Facebook to socialize, find entertainment and news, make comments, and read the news feeds of friends and sites they are following. Leading them away breaks up this continuity. People who might otherwise be a supporter or click "Like" on your campaign page may ignore your website altogether because they don't want to leave Facebook at that moment. If you still want to drive traffic to your website from the fan page, customize the ad so that users go directly to the fan page first, not to your website. From there, the content on your fan page, such posts, comments, status updates, event announcements, should include links to your campaign website. Supporters interacting with your fan page will naturally be inclined to visit your campaign website later.

A special type of Facebook ad is the 'Sponsored Stories' option, which allows any posts on your political fan page to be listed as an ad. Not only does this promote your Facebook page but it also promotes specific types of content on your page.

Both types of ads are pay-per-click, which means the campaign only spends money when someone clicks on the ad directly. Other Facebook users can still view the ad for free; even if visitors don't click on a political ad, they still see the message repeatedly, which can be advantageous for campaigns.

Campaigns can also customize Facebook ads to target members based on preferences listed on their profiles and overall demographics. The level of targeting can become very refined, so create different ads that are tailored to specific demographics (e.g. single women in their 30s can be one target group for a campaign that wants to highlight equality in the workplace).

Facebook also offers 'hypertargeting' within social networks. For example, when creating a campaign ad, you can choose to target only friends of people already connected with the campaign. Among circles of friends, the appeal of a cause or campaign is strong. Hypertargeting can amplify the reach and impact of your campaign's message by selecting this friends-of-friends option.

10. Announce events and ask for volunteers over Facebook.

Political engagement through Facebook really deepens once people go from being digital supporters to supporters on the ground, hosting events and mobilizing rallies and fundraising events. Don't be afraid of monitoring your top supporter and participants on the fan page and later soliciting them for help. These enthusiastic supporters are your campaign evangelists and often will be happy to lend a hand. Just as companies often do promotion programs through their Facebook fan pages, political campaigns can also offer giveaways, prizes and other incentives for encouraging supporters to go that extra mile.

11. Using Facebook to test different campaign strategies and messaging with "like" and share question option.

Facebook has also become a rich data source to test political campaign tactics. Between May and June 2011, SocialCode conducted a field experiment among Facebook users in Iowa and New Hampshire testing ad campaigns for seven Republican contenders for the Republican presidential nomination.[45] The Facebook users in these critical

---

45   "Study: GOP Facebook Ads Highly Influential for 2012", 13 June 2011, AllFacebook.com, http://www.allfacebook.com/study-gop-facebook-ads-highly-influential-for-2012-2011-06 (accessed 20 June 2011).

states were asked to click "Like" in response to randomly displayed image ads of the candidates (or a GOP elephant) with five common Republican messages (anti-Obama, healthcare, economy, values, and national security).

They found that Sarah Palin received the highest number of "Likes" across all five messages. Among the messages, while the 'Values' message ranked fourth among the five message option, it was the biggest driver of "Like" for Palin; the message focused on the economy in combination with Palin did not perform so well among the Facebook audience in those states. This suggests that voters do not associate her with the competence to address economic issues compared to the other Republican contenders. Among other contenders, Mitt Romney fared well in association with healthcare, despite his Massachusetts health plan.

SocialCode also found that the message that resonated the most in the ads was the message that directly opposed the Obama administration and agenda. Researchers concluded that Republican contenders should focus their messaging first on an anti-Obama slant, followed by healthcare and the economy. By state, Iowa saw the healthcare message perform as well as the Anti-Obama message, while New Hampshire citizens found that the healthcare message resonated better. By age, younger adults under 30 prioritized the economy. By gender, men responded better to the anti-Obama slant.

To make the most of Facebook as a testing tool, use the 'Share Question' option on your page. This lets you post questions and canvass your fans to find out everything from their thoughts on the issues you are campaigning about to getting their feedback on a campaign event you hosted. Not only will you generate ideas to improve your campaign strategy, but you will also generate conversation that will drive traffic to your page.

Twitter: The Campaign's Megaphone

Twitter is a micro-blogging service that allows users to send and read short, text-based messages that are displayed on a running newsfeed. Users expand their Twitter network by following other users and being followed by others. Followers of your Twitter newsfeed can see your tweets in reverse chronological order on the main Twitter page.

Compared to Facebook, which can be a cornucopia of content, Twitter is spare and economical. Limited to only 140 characters, each entry is the length of a headline. Tweets can link to longer, more detailed content, like articles and websites pages also. The blast of tweets can be addicting to users because they enable people to quickly scan ideas and topics. Popular ideas or trends are often 'tagged', which are made searchable by other users. For example, Obama's 2012 campaign tags certain tweets with the hashtag #obama2012 to refer to news and updates related to the re-election fight. Twitter also makes for quirky and witty quips that quickly go viral and spread through the Twitterverse.

Why it Matters

Twitter's growth as a political tool is no more apparent than during the 2009 Iranian elections, when anti-government groups used Twitter to stage protests and to disseminate information. The U.S. State Department even requested Twitter to put off scheduled maintenance to avoid disrupting the service and to keep Iranians and interested parties exchanging and spreading information about the elections. The former national security advisor, Mark Pfeifle has even called for Twitter to be nominated for the Nobel Peace Prize because "without Twitter the people of Iran would not have felt empowered and confident to stand up for freedom and democracy".[46]

Streams of tweets ring around the world with increasing intensity. Since the end of 2010, there are now more than 100 million Twitter users.[47] People are also becoming more open with the information they share according to a recent study by Sysomos, a social media monitoring and analytics technology firm. Users are also more willing to part with location information with 73 percent displaying this information compared to only 44 percent in 2009. The Sysomos report also found that Twitter users are consuming more tweets from people outside their circle of friends. Users with more than 100 friends increased three-fold between 2009 and 2010.

Twitter has become the communication of choice among politicians and public figures. Barack Obama made his 2008 victory announcement on Twitter. Republican candidates for the 2012 presidential election used Twitter to officially announce their runs for office.

Twitter decidedly takes on an active role during elections. While not covering any of the antics and news related to campaigns, such as Facebook, Twitter encouraged voters to report their experiences at the polling booth using various hashtags, such as #votereport and #NYCvotes for New York.[48] Twitter also encouraged people to broadcast their participation in the electoral process by using the hashtag #ivoted, which also encouraged followers in their networks to vote.

---

46 "Twitter Should Win Nobel Peace Prize", 7 July 2009, http://www.telegraph.co.uk/technology/twitter/5768159/Twitter-should-win-Nobel-Peace-Prize-says-former-US-security-adviser.html (accessed 20 June 2011).

47 Twitter, *Twitter Statistics for 2010 Report*, December 2010, http://www.sysomos.com/insidetwitter/twitter-stats-2010/ (accessed 20 June 2011).

48 "Social Media in the 2010 US Midterm Election: What Worked (And What Didn't)", 3 November 2010, http://socialtimes.com/social-media-in-the-2010-us-midterm-election-what-worked-and-what-didnt_b27242 (accessed 20 June 2011).

Strategies for Optimal Use

1. Use Twitter to find real-time information on what people are thinking about issues relevant to your campaign and candidacy.

Twitter is best used to find real-time information about an event or topic related to your campaign. Use its Search facility to gauge feedback about an event you just held such as a rally or voter mobilization kick-off. Hop on Twitter's search facility and see what people are saying about your candidacy or campaign. As your campaign builds followers, Twitter can be used as a forum for your campaign to post questions and get answers. You can ask your followers what they think about a campaign strategy and get feedback instantaneously. In essence, use Twitter as a monitoring tool for issues, trends, and events associated with your campaign. Twitter is essentially a newsfeed so it's easy to stay up-to-date on the latest developments and news that can enable you to run a nimble and responsive campaign. You can also use various Twitter apps such as TweetDeck that will enable you to track and monitor particular search strings.

2. Be a follower! Follow other people, organizations and new sites.

ABC Politics has a Twitter stream followed by many interested in political coverage. You can even narrow down what you monitor by following specific commentators. It's also always a good idea to monitor pundits with opposing points of view to see how your messages are being interpreted (or distorted) by the other side.

3. Use Twitter to communicate with your social network— and to fire them up!

According to Twitter, one of its key benefits is the ability to communicate casually with citizens, creating relationships of goodwill along the way—the equivalent of the digital handshake. As a communication tool, Twitter is an easy way to keep you connected with your supporters. Make sure your tweets are well-thought out and interesting. Avoid mundane tweets—if it reads like a press release you're going about it the wrong way. If you are highlighting more serious, text-heavy information, write a snappy, thought-provoking lead-in with your tweet and link to the more detailed information elsewhere.

Twitter is best used as a social media amplifier. Think of Twitter as your campaign's megaphone or the digital equivalent of letter-writing campaigns and protest groups chanting your campaign slogan. Twitter is a great way to mobilize supporters and keep the pressure on opponents. If your tweets are strong and interesting, your enthusiastic supporters will do the rest by retweeting your thoughts around the Twitterverse. Messages will spread rapidly across other networks of friends and family, pushing the message out farther afield.

In Canada, during the 2011 elections, messages from Green Party leader Elizabeth Moss and Liberal Leader Michael Ignatieff to Prime Minister Stephen Harper were retweeted by supporters. The digital chant placed pressure on the sitting government to recognize the opposition's take on the issues and demand for more public debate. There were more than 90,000 Twitter messages in the first week of the election alone. Ignatieff's gauntlet dropping "any time, any place" message was one of the more popular tweets, which challenged the sitting government to a one-on-one showdown.[49] Mitt Romney challenged Barack Obama on

---

49   "CTV 2011 Federal Election: Social Media Takes Off in First Week of Campaign", 2 April 2011, http://www.ctv.ca/servlet/ArticleNews/story/CTVNews/20110402/social-

Twitter by tweeting, "@barackobama I look forward to hearing details on your jobs plan, as are 14m unemployed Americans"— which was a big hit among his supporters.[50]

4. Use Twitter in creative ways to recognize supporters or to give them a more visible profile in your campaign.

As your supporters tweet about you, take the most interesting and eye-catching tweets and post them on your website or on Facebook. This spotlights bright moments in the frenzy of Twitter activity and makes your supporters feel as if they are directly part of the ongoing Twitter conversation. Send followers direct messages and thank them for following you. A steady stream of tweets promoting your campaign will follow and people will follow you more closely.

5. Use Twitter creatively to show off your political prowess and become a hero to your constituents.

During the December 2010 blizzard that swooped down over much of the Northeast, Cory Booker, the mayor of Newark New Jersey took to Twitter to help citizens in his town during the #snowpocalypse. By monitoring hashtags and Twitter streams of resident followers, Booker turned Twitter into a public-service tool. The mayor's Twitter account @CoryBooker was flooded with requests for help. The mayor monitored requests and took his team to the streets to where complaints were spilling over, armed with snowplows and shovels.

---

media-election-110402/20110402?s_name=election2011 (accessed 20 June 2011).

50   "Romney uses Twitter to Tweak Obama Announcement", 4 April 2011, http://www.boston.com/news/politics/politicalintelligence/2011/04/romney_uses_twi.html (accessed 20 June 2011).

Booker's own tweets about the experience were decidedly accessible and presented him as a concerned citizen ready to reach out to his neighbors. In one tweet, he said, "Just doug [sic] a car out on Springfield Ave and broke the cardinal rule: 'Lift with your Knees!!' I think I left part of my back back there."[51] Booker frantically drove around Newark using his Twitter feed as a radar to help people in need, offering everything from shoveling snow from driveways to buying diapers for moms shut-in without supplies for their kids.

Use Twitter as a direct conduit to engage citizens on a variety of issues relevant to your campaign. It can turn you into an instant political hero, someone who has his or her finger on the pulse of the people. While Twitter is useful to take a helicopter view of what people are ranting and raving about on the issues, it becomes an incomparable tool for commenting on what's happening on the ground. The publicity for your campaign in the Twitterverse is much better than a one-time photo-op for the newspapers.

6. Use Twitter to boost campaign research.

Twitter can be used as a tagging tool, enabling campaign staff to track where Twitter supporters are tweeting. This gives your campaign real-time, newsfeed views of what's happening on the ground in any particular place or time. This type of data is especially useful when monitoring reaction at campaign events, such as rallies or fundraisers, to get a sense of what supporters are feeling and responding to at an event. For example, if supporters demonstrate a rush of enthusiasm or excitement over a particular line in a speech— you can take a video clip

---

51   "Mayor Booker Uses Twitter to Aid New Jersey Blizzard Cleanup", 29 December 2010, Time magazine, http://www.time.com/time/nation/article/0,8599,2039945,00. html (accessed 20 June 2011).

of that moment or quote that text to be used for other promotional purposes. You can also capture and distill related footage and disseminate the media material on your campaign website or Facebook page.

Twitter's Annotations is a feature that categories tweets by 'type' and 'attribute'— tools that enable users to better sort through and search for tweets and analyze tweet trends.

7. Make strategic use of hashtags to get your campaign Twitter stream included in relevant searches.

Keeping an eye on various Twitter hashtags can help you monitor different insights and geographical, political and institutional takes on the electoral process and results. It serves as your campaign's pulse taker, letting you follow a variety of sources all at once and get links to coverage. By watching certain hashtags your campaign can get more involved in a direct way.

8. See what people are talking about and adjust your tweets to complement or contradict trending ideas.

Listen for references to your campaign. When someone says something nice about your candidacy or tweets information related to your campaign, be sure to pick up on it and retweet. Retweeting spreads the buzz and is an effective way for you to link your campaign to the wider Twitterverse conversation.

Negative comments should not be discounted outright. Your willingness to engage all respondents and participants demonstrates your trustworthiness and confidence as a political contender. In the eye of those who are still shopping around for a candidate, seeing less than perfect comments about your campaign ensures that you've been, in some way, properly 'vetted'. The public trusts the voice and opinion of others. In this way, Twitter builds your campaign as a trusted brand. It will get you noticed and keep your supporters retweeting and talking about you, keeping the conversation going and your campaign in the spotlight.

9. Try Twitter's 'Promoted Tweets' advertising feature.

Under the Promoted Tweets system, your campaign can buy your tweets rise to the top of search lists. For example, if you want a particular issue or idea to be promoted by Twitter, you could create a tweet triggered by keywords related to that issue. When users search on those keywords, your tweet will automatically appear at the top of search results identified with a label "Promoted Tweet". Twitter has devised a scoring system that evaluates how good your promoted tweet is. If it is constantly re-tweeted and clicked, it remains at the top perch in your search. If not, it will drop off into obscurity. Third party advertisers are no longer allowed to incorporate sponsored or paid messages into their Twitter feeds. Here are the key features of quality, sponsored tweets:

- **Keep it real. Be funny, clever, quirky, or pull at heartstrings.**

- **Make a powerful offer or make a big promise.**

- **Promote a social good or cause, which appeals to people's sense of civic duty.**

- **Meet a need for specialized information.**

10. Post regularly and frequently.

Twitter is a social media creature of voracious appetite. Because of its frantic pace, tweets quickly fall off news feeds. To keep your campaign visible, make sure to tweet at least several times a day. Frequent tweets are recommended during the times of the day when users are checking their Twitter feeds, such as the morning, noon, mid-afternoon, early evening and late evening. Plan a schedule of a 2:1 or 3:1 ratio of Twitter posts to Facebook posts. If you plan seven posts to Facebook per week, go for 15-20 posts on Twitter. Set up news alerts and mine sites that you monitor for campaign research and summarize interesting tidbits for tweets later. Be sure to tweet new blog articles that come out and noteworthy Facebook posts that deserve extra amplification and emphasis.

11. It's not only whom you know, but also whom you follow.

Following others quickly builds up your Twitter network, as people you follow will generally follow you back. Be sure to check out the networks of your followers of similar people you can also add to you network. But be discerning. Only add followers who have interests that align with your campaign vision or areas of expertise. While this is not a hard-and-fast rule, it will keep your network tight and focused so you'll know your messages are reaching the right people.

12. Establish an inspiring mission in your Twitter profile.

This can be your campaign's short and sweet pitch— a perspective that can be expressed in a few words and captures what you and your campaign are all about. Make sure you sound off on what's important to you and why you are running in the campaign.

13. Personalize the account.

While the Twitter handle and profile may refer only to the campaign or candidate, be sure to identify who manages your Twitter feed by name, e.g. "Tweets by [name]." Tweets directly by candidates should be signed as such.

LinkedIn: Social Networking Site Where You Can Press The Cyber Flesh

LinkedIn is a global professional network with over 100 million members. LinkedIn is regarded as the Rolodex of contacts, which makes it a great network for any political campaign to use to exchange information, ideas, and share and explore relevant issues.[52]

Why it Matters

Designed to be a business networking tool, LinkedIn's face value as a political tool may seem dim, but a recent study from the Pew Research Center shows that the networking site may be undervalued. As Facebook fans use Facebook for fun, turn to LinkedIn for a more focused type of networking and influence. The Pew study suggested that LinkedIn may be on the rise to becoming a new digital background for political campaigns. Researchers found that LinkedIn draws older, more educated citizens who are more apt to vote and are more consistent about their social and political leanings.[53] According to the study, LinkedIn users were the most politically-engaged among social network users, with 36 percent of members influencing others to vote (12 percentage points more than Facebook) and 79 percent reporting that they did or intended to vote (14 percentage points more than Facebook).

Compared to other social networking sites, LinkedIn is often overlooked by political campaigns as most politicos are focused on increasing the number of Facebook fans than LinkedIn connections. But be-

---

52   LinkedIn Learning Center, http://learn.linkedin.com/ (accessed 20 June 2011).

53   "Social Networking Sites and Our Lives", 16 June 2011, Pew Center Internet and American Life Project, http://pewInternet.org/Reports/2011/Technology-and-social-networks/Summary.aspx (accessed 20 June 2011)

cause of growth and activity among LinkedIn users, it may become the next untapped treasure trove for campaigns to place targeted advertising and form online discussion groups.

Strategies for Optimal Use

1. Engage with your Connections for information and for expertise.

LinkedIn is useful for campaigns looking to hire people for positions or seeking campaign consultants to tap for various projects. If campaigns are seeking people with special skills, the first place to go digging around for experts is LinkedIn. The site provides a trusted way to find the right people who fit the bill— a kind of convenient digital word-of-mouth.

For example, if you are looking for someone with social marketing skills who can spearhead your blogging efforts, check out LinkedIn for potential contacts with the background you need. Just run a search of profiles with those skills in a zip code you are in. Narrow down the search with keywords and political affiliations. LinkedIn is a good place to find your 'flock'.

LinkedIn is also a good place run a background check on people you are looking to hire for your campaign. It allows you to track where people came from (previous jobs and experience) and corroborate resumes that cross your desk.

2. Use LinkedIn for highly-targeted campaign messaging.

Because it is used exclusively as a professional networking tool, LinkedIn is, by nature, a more focused and discreet social media platform than Facebook or Twitter. Use LinkedIn to target specific groups or niches of constituents. Join a few Groups to show your affiliation with other professional networks, to embed yourself into various online discussions and to kick-off some interesting interactions with your supporters. In fact, there is a LinkedIn Group for the politically-minded. If anything, joining a group demonstrates some dimension of your candidacy that makes you tick as a professional.

Eventually, as your influence and number of Connections on LinkedIn grows, your campaign can consider starting its own Group page with your network. A LinkedIn Group is a great way to reach people and stay in touch with your supporters. LinkedIn users are already primed to network with others with similar interests and it can be a great way to find new audiences and supporters for your campaign.

3. Use LinkedIn to build a more comprehensive professional biography, beyond what's available on your web site.

Providing you a solid, searchable professional profile is where LinkedIn really excels among the social media platforms. Write a professional bio that serves as your business card with selling points and subtle insights to your stellar qualifications as a candidate. LinkedIn is a frequent resource for industry media, journalists, business leaders, and PR people— the crowd that could have the most influence on public opinions at the local and national levels. Help shape your public identity as a candidate by cultivating a complete and dynamic LinkedIn profile. A scantily-written LinkedIn profile conveys the impression of being a lightweight or someone who is behind the times and out of touch.

4. Update your status on a regular basis.

Just like Facebook, LinkedIn lets you update a status that shares with your connections and followers a new development in the campaign, your opinion on a particular issue or topic, or an announcement to rally supporters or invite people to attend an event. Updates anchor your campaign efforts in the professional worlds of your connections. Status updates on LinkedIn are also a perfect soapbox from which to broadcast your latest blogs.

TripIt is a handy application on LinkedIn that lets you log your travel schedule. If you have a busy travel schedule filled with various town hall meetings and stumping rallies, letting your connections know where you are gives people a chance to find out where they can reach you. It also alerts you to who among your connections is based in the city where you are campaigning. This is useful for any campaign that is looking to generate local interest or to organize meetings with local voters.

CAUTION: Don't overshare confidential campaign information— because the opposing side can mine it. Especially risky on LinkedIn is the chance of broadcasting information that may harm your campaign, such as strategy secrets, special plans or whereabouts, leaked press releases, premature releases of campaign news, disparaging news about the opposition, and so on. Make sure you have the information flow under control on LinkedIn and that your posts will not have negative repercussions down the road.

5. Use the Introductions feature.

To keep expanding your LinkedIn network, ask your Connections for introductions to other individuals, companies, groups, or geographical areas you want to reach. It's a great way to expand into unchartered territory and to increase the coverage and reach of your campaign.

Adding individuals as connections makes them feel like they know the candidate and with direct messaging a candidate can "press the cyber flesh" creating an illusion that the candidate and recipient are friends or connected.

6. Advertise on LinkedIn.

Buying ad space on LinkedIn gives you another platform to make your campaign more visible. With a membership that is a 100 million-strong and growing, and boasting older and wealthier members than you would find on Facebook or MySpace, LinkedIn could provide you access to a demographic that is a prime target for your campaign.

Using Video: Google/YouTube and Campaign Multimedia Options

In the 2008 presidential elections, contenders enlisted explicit social media platforms like Facebook and Twitter— but also took advantage of other digital tools available online, such as those offered by Google.

Why it Matters

Google owns YouTube and provides a massive audience (more than 80 million visitors per day) for any political messages you want to broadcast. If your campaign is considering a multimedia approach, Google's YouTube channels should not be overlooked. Here are several reasons why your campaign should be actively generating content for YouTube:

- **Going viral:** Among the types of media content available, video is one of the most passed-around formats on the web. When a particular video becomes popular, it can spread like wildfire as viewers post it on their Facebook pages, tweet about it, and e-mail it to their friends, family and colleagues. Videos can be inane footage, like silly pet home videos, or it can be startling and arresting imagery from a street protest in Egypt. During election cycles, political videos are an easy way to spread the news about candidates. In recounting her first introduction to Barack Obama during the 2008 presidential election, Rahaf Harfoush, author of Yes We Did, cites a YouTube video. She writes:[54]

---

54   Harfoush, Rahaf, 2009, Yes We Did: An Inside Look at How Social Media Built the Obama Brand (Berkeley: New Riders), p. xii-xiii.

I remembered when I received a link to the same video from three different friends…and noticed the buzz on both Twitter and Facebook…Shot in black and white, the video featured musical artist, Will.i.am from the Black Eyed Peas accompanied by a slew of celebrities singing along to one of Barack Obama's speeches. It wasn't the faces of the rich and famous that had me sitting up. It was the message of hope and change coming from a man that until that moment I had only studied from a distance…The refrain "Yes We Can", Obama's concession speech from the New Hampshire primary, had been put to music. I remember feeling a shiver as I watched that video. It moved me, and I shared it with all my family and friends…That video was a wake-up call, the catalyst that would lead me to join one of the world's most historic political campaigns."

- **Search visibility:** Search engines, like Google, make all types of content, not just web pages, available within search results. So if you search on a political candidates name, the search results will include blog posts, news items, and images from videos posted to YouTube or other video sharing sites, such as Vimeo. Videos are often prominently displayed, so users have the option of just browsing uploaded videos. If your campaign is not using videos, it is losing out on a great amount of potential web traffic from search results.

- **Inbound links** to raise page rank: Finally, when your campaign is focused on building page rank on search engines, know that uploading videos to sites like YouTube allows you to take advantage of the traffic and high page rank of the site. First upload your video to YouTube, preferably to your own political channel. Then, embed a copy of the video (YouTube automatically gives you the embed code to use) to your own campaign website or blog. Videos can serve as 'link bait' for viewers who watch your video and embed it in their own blogs and sites. External links build up your page rank and improve your search rankings among the major search engines.

Strategies for Optimal Use

1. Explore Google's Political Toolkit

Google offers free and paid multimedia services and tools for political campaigns, mostly through YouTube at YouChoose.

- **YouTube Political Channel.** Campaigns can come here to list an official political channel on YouTube. Providing a central directory of all campaign channels available, the site serves as a YouTube 'home base' for campaigns. By listing here, campaigns enhance their 'brand' to the public and access more video functionality, such as uploads for longer videos and custom thumbnail selection for your videos.

  To qualify for the YouTube Political Channel, make sure you: 1) Qualify with the Board of Elections for your state or Federal Election Commission to get on the ballot for the political office you intend to run for; 2) Demonstrate that you have a measurable level of public support for your campaign already, which YouTube will assess by looking at your volunteer staff, poll results, and news coverage of your campaign; 3) Prove that you are making an active campaign effort (YouTube will check the existence of your campaign office, a staff, and phone number, a fully operational and active fundraising arm, and campaign schedule).

- **YouTube Moderator:** Use the Moderator feature on YouTube with your political channel to engage with your viewers and make your videos truly interactive. When enabled, viewers can post comments, questions, or ideas on your YouTube channel. Moderator makes it easy for campaigns to leverage the collective wisdom of the crowd and participate in conversations with supporters. To use Moderator, decide on a topic or focus. Determine how you want to collect responses, such as— questions for an online interview, feedback for an event, or fundraising ideas. Define what you want your audience to contribute and be sure to respond to popular submissions. In political campaigns and forums in the past, Moderator has been used to: 1) collect questions for a YouTube interview with President Obama in the 'Your State of the Nation' channel; 2) Gather money savings tips from the community to help ease budgets during the recession; and 3) Engage foreign leaders at the World Economic Forum at Davos.

- **YouTube Insight:** Campaigns can use YouTube's Insights analytical tools to evaluate video performance and find out information on viewers. Campaigns can also track the source of traffic— whether it's from embedded links, search, or external sites like blogs and other web sites.

2. Use Google Ad Words to create promoted videos.

Promoted videos are a form of paid advertising that Google offers. Campaigns purchase keywords and search terms for spots on YouTube search results. Payment is pay-per-click, which means you only spend money when viewers click your ad.

Google Ads are behaviorally targeted. They're served-up based on what someone's actually doing online. For instance, Google search ads will show up on search results based on keywords entered. Likewise, Google content ads appear on websites (like Epolitics.com) tied to the actual words on the page— a page about politics, for instance, would feature political ads. So, a reader will only see ads on a given topic if he or she has chosen to read a page that's related to that topic.

3. Use Call-to-Action overlays to link from videos to your website.

Overlays allow a campaign to add a message or call-to-action to their Promoted videos. The message appears as soon as the video begins. Use the overlay to ask your viewers to visit your campaign website or blog, or use it to make a fundraising pitch or to visit other videos in your political channel. Users can close the overlay to continue watching your video or click it to be directed to a specified overlay destination URL. The overlay feature is free and can be deactivated later.

4. It's YouTube, not boob tube.

A lot of campaigns make the mistake of posting videos on YouTube or other video sites and leaving it at that. Avoid turning it into a passive viewing experience for viewers. Keep the conversation and buzz going about your video content by making sure you respond to comments. Make sure to add your campaign views on footage to elicit responses and discussion.

5. Add as much content as possible.

Google recommends you 'flood the system' with as much relevant footage as possible. Upload the usual clips from speeches and TV appearances, as well as the more behind-the-scenes footage from your campaign. Make sure you continuously feed new and original material to your video feed or political channel and keep clips under five minutes to avoid losing interest.

6. Distribute your videos on other social media platforms.

E-mail your video to supporters, embed them on your blog or website, and post them on your Facebook page and Twitter feed. Spreading the word is important to get the ball rolling and to reach everyone beyond the YouTube community.

7. Stay authentic and true.

Focus on uploading video content that is compelling and authentic. Avoid the temptation to use YouTube or other video hosting sources to recycle and rebroadcast videos that are too much like TV ads. Overly political messages will fall flat and turn viewers away. Choose footage that employs more relaxed, personal dialogue, and natural conversation. Google recommends these types of videos for maximum impact:[55]

---

55   Google, YouChoose2010 Tip Sheet, http://www.youtube.com/pdf/Tips_ YouChoose2010.zip (accessed 20 June 2011).

- **Q&A:** Create a question and answer series, in which you respond to video ideas and questions from the YouTube community.

- **Fundraising impact:** Show how campaign donations are being used and use call-to-action overlays to drive supporters to your external donation page.

- **Thematic stories:** Create episodic content related to themes from your campaign.

- **Responses to current events:** Create videos of your candidate expressing views on breaking news and other current events.

- **Endorsements:** Record testimonials from celebrities and other high-profile public figures.

- **Opposition footage:** Show clips of your opposition giving speeches or giving campaign appearances and counter with your own arguments to foster debate.

- **Campaign trail:** Film behind-the-scenes footage of the campaign trail.

8. Check out Google's other online tools, like Google Docs, Google Reader, and Google Alerts.

Google Docs had a profound influence on campaign operations during the 2008 presidential elections, though it received the least amount of publicity. What Google Docs facilitated with its features was online collaboration. In a social space where grassroots campaigns are born

and nurtured on the web, online collaboration became the central catalyst to making social networks work for your campaign.

Practical ways Google Docs can be used in political campaigns include:

- **Provides an easy way to revise content.** Campaign
  staffers have a seamless way to fine-tune and work on
  speeches, press releases, blog articles, and keep track of
  versions.

- **Makes data-sharing fast and secure.** A document started
  in campaign headquarters could make its rounds to
  satellite offices for input and revisions with ease.

- **Reduces risk of mistakes tracking event attendance.**
  Sign-up and attendance sheets at rallies and events can
  be reconstituted online, reducing the risk of being lost or
  corrupted in some way.

Google Reader also allows users to subscribe to favorite websites
to get new content instantly. Campaigns can use Google Reader to keep
track of campaign news, relevant keywords such as your candidate's
name, on news sites as well as favorite blogs or other media sites. Campaigns can even subscribe to pre-packaged bundles on popular topics
for easy access.

Google Alerts is a service, which notifies its users by e-mail, or as a feed, about user preferred web and news pages. Google currently offers several types of alert searches: "News", "Web", "Blogs", "Comprehensive", "Video" and "Groups".[56]

- **A news alert** is an email that lets the user know if new articles make it into the top 10 results of his/her Google News search.

- **A web alert is** an email that lets the user know if new web pages appear in the top 20 results for his/her Google Web search.

- **A News and Web alert** is an email that lets the user know when new articles related to his/her search term make it into the top 10 results for a Google News search or the top 20 results for a Google Web search.

- **A Groups alert** is an e-mail that lets the user know if new posts make it into the top 50 results of his/her Google Groups search.

---

56   Agranoff, Craig and Tabin, Herb, 2010, Do It Yourself Online Reputation Management: A Step-By-Step Guide To Building Or Repairing Your Online Reputation (Pendant Publishing).

Advanced Tools: Expanding your Social Pulpit

Once you have the basics down, it's time to move to a Social Media 2.0 approach in integrating digital strategies to your campaign. Here, you'll take your program to the next level by integrating more advanced tools in strategic ways, as well as learning how to pull it all together in a seamless digital program.

Mobile Technologies: Campaigning on the Go

The digital experience of social media and the web are no longer anchored to your desk or even laptop— and are moving toward your mobile phones or tablets, ensuring that we stay always connected, even on the go. Smart phones and other mobile devices have evolved into useful points of contact for political campaigns to rally activists and supporters to various events. Text messages can be 'blasted' to large groups of people to announce last minute changes in logistics or to organize local flash mobs in particular locations with agility and speed.

This strategy was deployed most frequently by Obama during the 2008 presidential campaign and by Senator Scott Brown of Massachusetts during his 2010 election campaign. Bigger campaigns like the ones run by Senator Harry Reid of Nevada and California Republicans Carly Fiorina and Meg Whitman were able to design their own apps that gave supporters instant access to campaign information.

With more than 55 million Americans using smart phones, the potential is tremendous for political campaigns. One area where there is untapped potential is advertising. Americans spend a significant portion of their day with their mobile phones at hand, which means 6-10 hours a day where you can grab the attention of potential voters. Yet in 2010, political campaigns spent only 1 percent of their advertising budgets on mobile advertising.[57] According to marketing research firm comScore, this lack of attention is mostly due to demographics. More than half of smart phone users in the U.S. are between the ages of 18-34, a group that is seen as unreliable voters or who are thought to be better reached directly through social media platforms, such as Facebook and Twitter. Many ignore the fact that smart phones now host apps that let people access those social media sites. Many naysayers also say that the audience for smart phone ads is self-selected. While they may encourage rank-and-file supporters to head to the polls and vote favorably for candidates, they do little to sway undecided voters.

Why it Matters

Digital media strategists point out untapped opportunities for campaigns to reach more people through mobile platforms and advertising, which have a deeper reach and cost less than traditional advertising on television. Republican campaigns in particular are exploring mobile ads. According to Eric Frenchman, chief Internet strategist at Republican consulting firm Connell Donatelli, "I think the campaigns that are running [mobile ads] now are going to get paid dividends in November." [58]

---

57   "Smart-phone ads not yet political", 24 October 2010, Politico, http://www.politico. com/news/stories/1010/44078.html (accessed 20 June 2011).

58   "Smart-phone ads not yet political", 24 October 2010, Politico, http://www.politico. com/news/stories/1010/44078.html (accessed 20 June 2011).

GPS-based Data Mining and Geo-Tagging

According to Jonathan Askin, a media expert at Brooklyn Law School, one of the biggest leaps in savvy social media use came during 2008 presidential election with the use of mobile technology— specifically location-based services and data mining for targeted marketing through mobile-based tools.[59]

In fact, a significant volume of interaction from voters (click-through-rates) can be coursed and channeled through mobile devices through 'mobile surges'. Using GPS components on smart phones, campaigns can select specific zip codes or even selected city blocks and areas to direct their mobile ad campaigns. Google's mobile ads app can be used by campaigns to draw boundaries around areas they want to target on a sleek, interactive map.

During the summer months of 2010, Republican Michele Bachmann of Minnesota used GPS (global positioning system) data to blast ads to voters within specific areas. During the Minnesota State Fair, her campaign launched a geo-targeted online video campaign that sent people located within 10 kilometers of the fairgrounds links to YouTube videos. The videos criticized her Democratic opponent Tarryl Clark of allegedly raising taxes on popular state fair foods, such as beer, corn, hotdogs, and bacon.[60] Originally, the ad was scheduled to run while the State Fair was taking place as TV commercials, but the campaign decided a more powerful strategy would be to get the ad in front of fairgoers while they

59   "New Social media and the 2012 Election: Waaaaay Beyond Facebook 2008", 20 April 2011, Christian Science Monitor, http://www.csmonitor.com/USA/Society/2011/0420/New-social-media-and-the-2012-election-Waaaaay-beyond-Facebook-2008 (accessed 20 June 2011).

60   "How Rep. Michele Bachmann Used Mobile Ads to Turn Beer and Corn Dogs Into Votes From Fair Folk", 27 October 2010, Fast Company, http://www.fastcompany.com/1698173/mobile-poli-techs-how-rep-michelle-bachmann-used-mobile-ads-to-turn-beer-and-corn-dogs-into- (accessed 20 June 2011).

were physically at the fair itself. The mobile ads caused a stir and drew support from people who were attending fair activities. Later, analysts found that more than 60 percent of ad views came from Android and iPhone smart phones.

Foursquare, QR Codes, and other Location-Based Services

One challenge of political marketing is said to be turning online enthusiasm for a candidate to boots on the ground— hopefully walking to polls. In the past, get-out-the-vote efforts depended on door-to-door, telephone, and mail reminders. Now these efforts can be streamlined with location-based check-ins through services like Foursquare or through the use of QR codes, which can verify if voters have voted.

Why it Matters

This ability to check-in to a physical location, bringing together the offline and online worlds, offers creative ways for campaigns to leverage social media for future elections and campaigns. Republican candidate Tim Pawlenty made headlines by rolling out a digital campaign strategy that makes use of Foursquare.[61] In late 2010, Google launched its marketing experiment called "Goggles". Goggles aim was to leverage mobile phone technology to provide users a deeper and richer experience from print ads.[62]

---

61   "In 2012, a new world for online campaigning", 10 April 2011, StarTribune.com, http://www.startribune.com/politics/national/119575059.html?page=1&c=y (accessed 20 June 2011).

62   "What Google Goggles will do for the ad industry", 16 November 2010, Fast Company, http://www.fastcompany.com/1703045/how-augmented-reality-and-google-goggles-can-do-mazin-things-for-the-advertising-industry (accessed 20 June 2011).

Foursquare is a popular mobile phone app that uses geo-tagging technology to let you 'check-in' when you are at certain locations. By checking-in, you alert your friends where you have been or where you currently are located. The app now rewards you with points and special offers when you check in at local businesses, such as restaurants or coffee shops. Many have dubbed Foursquare the 'new Twitter', by creating new footholds in location-based services and making use of social media.[63] By encouraging people to broadcast their locations on Twitter and Facebook, Foursquare incentivizes users to visit and support certain business establishments. The more people visit a venue, the more buzz is generated about it on social media sites.

Using your smart phone, users can scan a print ad's QR code, which would enable access to a site for more information and even discounts and deals. The use of 'hidden content' provides campaigns another way to attract supporters by providing incentives to view ads and participate in surveys or to attend events.

---

63   "New Year's Twitter", 19 November 2009, CNN.com, http://www.cnn.com/2009/TECH/11/19/cashmore.foursquare/index.html (accessed 20 June 2011).

Strategies for Optimal Use

Campaigns can take advantage of location-based services in several ways:

1. Broadcast where you have support from local businesses and establishments.

Local campaigns can especially benefit from this strategy by working with small businesses where they ask for signs to be displayed in support of their candidacy.[64] When users visit the establishment and check-in using Foursquare, they would then receive a message that announces the establishment's support for a candidate or campaign. The message could include a link to more information about the campaign, which users could access on their mobile phones. Once on the site, users can then choose to give their mobile numbers or e-mail addresses to the campaign.

2. Create strategic partnerships with local residents and 'regulars'.

Collaborate with the popular visitors to establishments, dubbed by Foursquare as 'mayors' of a locale. These Foursquare mayors could be asked to co-host an event and invite members of his or her network to attend.

---

64 "Foursquare for Local Campaigns", 19 March 2010, Local PoliTechs, http://www.localpolitechs.com/2010/03/19/foursquare-local-campaigns/ (accessed 20 June 2011).

3. Streamline attendance and check-in tracking.

Foursquare and QR codes can also be used to keep track of volunteers and identify who are the most active. Campaigns can ask volunteers to check-in every time they make a visit to headquarters or other satellite campaign areas. Rewards to top volunteers could be built-in to Foursquare or QR check-ins to encourage more use. For example, supporters who use mobile check-ins at events can earn special rewards for their attendance, such as t-shirts, free food and drinks.

4. Track how many of your declared supporters on other social media platforms are attending offline events and rallies.

With the ascendance of location-based services and integration with mobile phones, Foursquare and QR codes could be used by campaigns to crosscheck and track who has attended rallies and fundraising events, and which events are the most popular. It also lets you see which of your supporters are the most gung-ho and determine areas that are saturated with support and those areas that rouse only lukewarm enthusiasm.[65] With access to this kind of powerful data, campaigns can adjust their strategies with more agility and flexibility.

---

65 "Why Location Will be the Killer App of the 2012 Elections", 1 May 2011, Mashable.com, http://mashable.com/2011/05/01/2012-election-killer-app/ (accessed 20 June 2011).

5. Combine location-based services with other media platforms and launch creative campaigns.

Campaigns could design virtual scavenger hunts to draw in support and participation. Visual recognition and scanning of QR codes on billboards, posters, flyers, and other print ads provide interesting ways political campaigns combine multiple media platforms.

6. Remind and encourage supporters to vote.

In response to check-ins, get-out-the-vote campaigns could target stragglers among supporters. Political campaigns can use it strategically to rally their supporters and push and prod more lukewarm voters. In 2010, Foursquare documented civic participation through its location services on its "I Voted" site, which was similar to the Facebook "I Voted" button.[66]

---

66 Foursquare 'I Voted', http://elections.foursquare.com/about/ (accessed 20 June 2011).

Flickr and Picasa:
Power of Photosharing for Campaigns

Pictures and images are powerful tools that all campaigns should harness. Pictures speak a thousand words. They have emotional impact and an ability to bring people together. Seeing images of supporters at a rally can have profound influence on how a campaign is perceived. Sharing photos of their participation in a campaign also makes people feel a sense of accomplishment; they feel they are part of something bigger. Most importantly pictures are very valuable in search and what appears in a search of you related to images.

Photosharing sites like Flickr and Picasa offer a glimpse of your campaign to supporters. It piques curiosity and interest and reveals an intimate look behind-the-scenes of your candidate. During the 2008 presidential election, the Obama campaign asked its supporters to share and post photos taken at events on Flickr and Picasa, another popular photo-sharing site. It amassed 660,315 photos on Flickr alone.

Strategies for Optimal Use

1. Invite your supporters to submit photos.

On Flickr or Picasa, set up groups related to your campaign. For example, you can set up a group related to campaign rallies, or a group related to candidate interviews. Ask your supporters to upload photos in the relevant groups. You can take the best photos and highlight them on your blog or website. When people are asked to participate in a directed way, they are more apt to feel more attached and supportive. [67]

---

67   "Creating a Flickr of interest for advocacy campaigns", 9 September 2009, http://www.mediabullseye.com/mb/2009/09/creating-a-flickr-of-interest.html (accessed 20 June 2011).

2. Be creative in rewarding your supporters for submitting photos.

In 2010, GE launched a digital campaign promoting environmental awareness that encouraged people to share their 'green ideas' by uploading photos on Flickr. For every photo of wind in action that was uploaded to Flickr, 4.5 kilowatt hours of wind energy was donated to Practical Action, a nonprofit focused on supporting solutions to fighting poverty; for water photos, GE donated 480 gallons to charity:water, a nonprofit dedicated to bringing clean and safe drinking water to people in developing countries; and every light photo triggered a donation of 175 hours of solar power to d.Light Lighting Oecusse Project, a nonprofit working to provide access to electricity to poor households around the world.[68] GE's campaign generated interest, public good will, and lots of publicity.

Conduct contests and ask supporters to take photos of their local campaign activities and post them on a Flickr or Picasa group.[69] Hold competitions for the best photo montage around certain themes, such as 'Unique ways to Fundraise' or 'Why I plan to vote'. Prizes like t-shirts, mugs and buttons are also a great incentive to reward your supporters for submitting photos but the possibility of a one-on-one meeting with the candidate is probably the ultimate incentive to drive photos to your page.

---

68   "GE Campaign Turns YouTube Videos and Flickr Photos into Clean Energy", 21 October 2010, Mashable.com, http://mashable.com/2010/10/21/ge-tag-your-green/ (accessed 20 June 2011).

69   "Creating a Flickr of interest for advocacy campaigns", 9 September 2009, http://www.mediabullseye.com/mb/2009/09/creating-a-flickr-of-interest.html (accessed 20 June 2011).

3. Give your staffers cameras and ask them to take photos.

Photography enthusiasts will tell you about the importance of having a camera ready because you never know what's going to happen. At an event, snap a photo. During the interview, get a shot of the candidate ruminating over his or her notes. Supporters love these intimate shots and appreciate being given a peek at these unofficial, ad-lib off-camera moments.

4. Tag your photos to monitor activity and to group together related photos.

Flickr and Picasa allow you to specify keywords and tags for uploaded photos, making it easier for users to find related photos. Make sure you give your supporters options to tag, add descriptions and categorize their photos. Maybe the tag, 'healthcare rally', is frequently used. Tagging lets you monitor what category of photos are the most popular, which may lead you to adjust your campaign strategies accordingly and be reflected as well.

Social Media Aggregators: A Crash Course

One-stop social media aggregators make it easy to update and keep track of your different social media platforms from a single central tool. Their column style format silos your information into different categories based on the number of accounts you maintain (e.g. Facebook fan page, Twitter account, etc.)

HootSuite

HootSuite is a web-based (no messy installation required!) robust tool that any campaign should consider for its social media aggregator of choice. Users can connect to several social media accounts from the application's column-based dashboard. Currently, there is support for Twitter, Facebook Pages, LinkedIn, Ping.fm, Wordpress.com, MySpace and Foursquare— a list that covers your basic and not-so-basic social media platforms. Users can also push their posts on several platforms and accounts at once. Being able to schedule posts on several sites can be a timesaver for many campaigns who want to broadcast announcements universally. Try their free version or pay $5.99 a month for unlimited statistics, Google analytics integration, Facebook Insights integration, and an advertising free space.

Here are the key features that will enable your campaign to track and manage its social media content:

- **Schedule options:** Post live updates to your various feeds or pre-schedule and stagger the release of posts and shares.

- **Customize URLs:** Setting custom link parameters enable you to track clicks and gather information from your supporters and visitors.

- **File upload:** Add images, video, and other files into your posted messages.

- **RSS feed:** Link to your RSS and send your blog posts right into your social media streams.

- **Hootlet:** A bookmark feature that can be installed on your browser. Click the icon from your browser while you are on a webpage and edit the tweet, Facebook post or Foursquare share in a pop-up window. Publish the content on different accounts and post live or at a scheduled time.

- **Mobile integration:** Get updates on your mobile phone.

- **Tabbed layout:** Harness the various streams from the social media platform into various sections, such as news, keywords, friends and more.

TweetDeck

TweetDeck originally pegged itself as a tool primarily for users of Twitter but it has since evolved into a broad base for other social media platforms, such as Facebook, LinkedIn and MySpace. TweetDeck is also available for your desktop and smartphones. TweetDeck uses Adobe Air to function, therefore it is a massive resource hog and slower to load than other aggregators, such as HootSuite.

Tweetdecks features are extensive and built around the principles that make Twitter so powerful:

- **Filters:** Lets you limit what you want to know. Great for zeroing-in on certain topics or issues related to your campaign. (For example want to know when a candidate is mentioned in a tweet? Add this filter and know within seconds when their name is tweeted.)

- **Trend-watch:** Allows you to see what's popular on Twitter and Twitscoop.

- **Photo integration options:** TweetDeck gives you three different Twitter photo services to choose from when integrating your photos into your posts or tweets.

- **URL shorteners:** Uses bit.ly to auto-shorten long URLs.

- **Twitter lists:** Let's you organize Twitter lists right on the dashboard.

- **Follower maintenance:** Follow and unfollow accounts from the TweetDeck dashboard.

- **Section layout:** Single page view of all your social media accounts.

Other Key Lessons For Making It All Work

With the variety and range of social media platforms out there, it will be challenging for any political campaign to orchestrate the available options into a unified strategy. Faced with so many tools, we have essentially a 'Goldilocks Dilemma'— if a campaign over reaches, it can risk diluting its political brand; if it underutilizes social media tools, it risks ignoring an area where a large segment of the population works and plays.

Joe Rospars, Obama's chief digital strategist and mastermind of the 2008 digital blowout, has said that the campaign that will be most successful with social media in the 2012 election will be the campaign that "integrates all the various elements of the digital channel— email, text, website, mobile apps, and social networks— together as one digital program, and also mixing the digital program together with the offline reality of field organizations."[70]

Here are several best practices for integrating your social media platforms into a unified digital strategy, both online and offline:

1. Consolidate your message from an online epicenter (e.g. use your website as the central platform for your campaign).

As the saying goes, 'All roads lead to Rome'; in the same way, all your social media platforms should link back to a central digital footprint, this will be your campaign website. Turn your campaign website into a resource center. It should be the place to go for your supporters to grab text, images, infographics, and audio and digital content to further spread the campaign message and brand on their own social media platforms.

Obama's 2008 MyBO website offered supporters a treasure trove of information, including videos, speeches, photos, and even how-to guides that provided the building blocks for any ordinary citizen to create their own personalized content supporting Obama's candidacy. *The Results:* Supporters created more than 400,000 pro-Obama videos and posted them to YouTube. They also wrote more than 400,000 blog posts as members on the MyBO Web site.

Use your website to address all of the long-tail issues your voters care about and speak directly to the constituents you want to represent. Provide links to all your online 'field offices' on social media platforms (e.g. Facebook, Twitter, YouTube, Flickr, etc.) and tailor the content on each of those sites to your audience.

---

70   "Barack Obama 2012 Campaign To Go Beyond Email, Text", 28 June 2011, The Huffington Post, http://www.huffingtonpost.com/2011/06/28/barack-obama-2012-campaign_n_886280.html?ir=Technology (accessed 20 June 2011).

2. Create low barriers to action and ensure online user action delivers tangible objectives.

In the final analysis, your digital media strategy is a means to an end— getting people to vote or support your campaign in the voter's booth. When used successfully, support on social media platforms is turned into the offline reality of making donations, volunteering to knock on doors and making phone calls, and finally, persuading people to vote and to vote in your favor. According to many experts, what you do online should complement your 'press-the-flesh' campaign strategies. The difference with social media is that you can capture those handshakes and smiles at rallies— and upload them on YouTube, tweet the pictures, tag them on your Flickr stream, and post them on Facebook.

3. Allow engagement at all levels.

The great thing about social media is that it allows you to capture both the casual and ardent supporter and lets you engage those two types of voters in different ways. Not every voter cares equally about every issue and each social media site's analytics should help you assess what particular topics resonate with different groups throughout the campaign.

Use social media platforms to drive up the intensity of support and commitment by offering more value for people's time and money. The Obama 2012 campaign has rehashed some of its more successful fundraising pitches, "offering small donors a chance to win a dinner with Obama and Biden and matching the contributions of $5 or more from first-time donors."[71] Taking advantage of the "birther outcry", the cam-

---

71   "Barack Obama 2012 Campaign To Go Beyond Email, Text", 28 June 2011, The Huffington Post, http://www.huffingtonpost.com/2011/06/28/barack-obama-2012-campaign_n_886280.html?ir=Technology (accessed 20 June 2011).

paign offered supporters a "Made in the USA" mug, with a picture of Obama's birth certificate on the back for those who donate $15 or more.

4. Be relevant and authentic, engage and add value to conversations.

Actively listen to your audience and participants and respond with thoughtfulness. Find ways to regularly engage with voters on a daily basis. Having you respond to their questions is not only personally satisfying for people, but also demonstrates to their friends and followers watching the exchange that you are involved.

Case Study: Obama's personal touch – how to connect with your supporters in a personal way

In the 2008 U.S. presidential election, the Obama camp set themselves apart from Clinton and later McCain by taking a more personal approach to social media. In an 'Ask Yahoo' event, the three political titans were asked to do a forum with its 60 million subscribers. The candidates logged on posted a question to the community.

Clinton got over 38,000 people to post their ideas and asked that the community vote for the best response. At first glance, the engagement was on par, Clinton's campaign engaged people well and then turned the tables around and empowered the people to vote for the best response. A thrilling experience for those involved but Clinton's camp dropped the ball when she responded on the process rather dryly in her official blog. She gave a cookie-cutter 'Thank you', adding, "she was moved by the poignant stories and impressed by the power and creativity."

McCain also gave automated-like responses to his 16,000 responses to his question. He told voters that he would "make it a top priority to balance the budget and bring fiscal discipline and accountability to a budget process that was badly broken." Sounds presidential and is great for a prepared speech— but not for this type of Q&A platform. It was riddled with canned buzz words and devoid of personality.

Like the others, Obama selected the best response to his posted question, but took a more personal approach in responding to participants. Rather than posting a response on site and thanking the participants, Obama called the person with the winning question. They spoke together on the phone briefly about engaging people in the political process.

His campaign recorded the conversation and posted it on their blog and various social networking profiles such as Facebook. Obama's strategy created an intimacy and genuine personal interest that was absent in the either Clinton's or McCain's reactions.

Key Points: Listen to members, identify key touchpoints in the conversation, and respond in a genuine manner.

The forum was a rather large, unwieldy process— with candidates fielding thousands of responses. But Obama made it feel like a special one-on-one event. With the personal phone call, he only connected directly with one person— but one person was all it took. People who didn't get a personal call from the Senator were drawn to the possibility that they *could* have been that person. The feeling among millions was, "Obama reached out to her. Well, he could reach out to me, too."

Marketers have always known this. Creating a personalized online experience can build a positive relationship between a consumer and your political brand.

5. Focus on the community.

The Obama 2008 presidential campaign was a political campaign like no other— stopping the business-as-usual political machine in its tracks and forever changing the way campaigns connected with voters and supporters. Part of its popularity stemmed from the decision to run a completely different kind of campaign, one that was buttressed by a new type of supporter: online communities.

Case Study: Creating online communities

Before the launch of MyBarackObama.com, Obama's official 2008 campaign website, social networking sites were abuzz with excitement. In just a day after the official announcement, more than 1,000 groups were created using the site's online tools. Even as the campaign was still gearing up and the site was being tweaked, the digital universe was already brimming with groups, blogs, fundraising pages, and events.

Early supporters used the MyBarackObama.com site as their platform of choice to extend what they were already doing on the ground and to connect and advertise to their own personal networks.

The Results: amplification of the Obama campaign to viral-levels. One such group that piggybacked off Obama site was Students for Barack Obama, which would go on to host over 19,000 events and raised $1.7 million with web outreach that supported efforts on the ground.

Chapter 5

How Not To Ruin Your Political Campaign

WITH THE emergence of social media, campaigns have found a new venue to put across their platform, ideology, and their stand on pressing issues of the world today. However, using social media is a tricky business. Unlike the use of print, such as in campaign posters, which can be torn down if found foolish, anything you throw into the digital realm can be captured, copied, and reincarnated over and over again. To ensure political longevity, it's best for campaigns to minimize digital blunders (or if possible, not have any at all!) or have a team on standby that can do damage control.

There are a lot of ways to harness the power of social media but a single misstep can bring down a whole campaign. Here are several gaffes to watch out for:

1. Refusing to acknowledge the power and efficacy of social media.

"A business with no sign is a sign of no business". Unfortunately, this holds true for politicians who have no online presence. How can a candidate say he is in touch with the public or his constituents if he has not harnessed the power of everyday social tools? McCain made the mistake of admitting that he was still a stranger to e-mail.[72] The "Still" ad ran by Obama's 2008 presidential campaign depicted John McCain as someone who was out of touch with the times.

With a country clamoring for change and in the middle of an economic depression, the public was looking for someone dynamic and forward-thinking. McCain's lack of digital finesse came across that he was a candidate who was out of touch, even clueless. If misuse of social media can hurt a campaign, having no understanding or sense of your social media strategy, can cause you the presidency. [73]

2. Recycling campaign slogans and talking points.

The voting public wants to hear authentic views, not be spoon-fed canned statements. This high-tech spamming on social media sites is called 'astroturfing' and was done by John McCain in the 2008 presidential race. McCain torpedoed his own campaign by posting comments and pronouncements that sounded like computer-generated press releases. Here's one notorious example: [74]

---

72   "Still Ad", 11 September 2008, http://www.youtube.com/watch?v=bQ2I0t_Twk0 (accessed 23 June 2011)

73   "Barack Obama vs. John McCain Social Media and Search Engine Scorecard", 5 November 2008, http://adultaddstrengths.com/2008/11/05/obama-vs-mccain-social-media/ (accessed 23 June 2011).

74   "Why McCain's Social Media Astroturfing Didn't Work", 9 September 2008, http://socialmediatoday.com/speakmediablog/106280/why-mccains-social-media-astroturfing-didnt-work (accessed 31 May 2011).

--- ▪ ▪ ▓ ▓ ▪ ---

"John McCain has a comprehensive economic plan that will create millions of good American jobs, ensure our nation's energy security, get the government's budget and spending practices in order, and bring relief to American consumers. Click to learn how the McCain Economic Plan will help bring reform, prosperity and peace to America."

--- ▪ ▪ ▓ ▓ ▪ ---

These generic statements only amplified a perception that the campaign lacked imagination and he was out of touch with the public and to make matters worse, this scripted post was posted again and again on social networking sites, giving it the odious whiff of spam.

3. Forgetting to build your fan base.

In July 2008, the McCain campaign launched a Facebook parody website called BarackBook.com that was supposed to be a play on the critical scrutiny of Barack Obama's questionable political connections.[75] It backfired, as it showed a complete lack of understanding of social networking fundamentals. In fact the site only garnered less than 200 fans. Every time a post was made to BarackBook, the Republican National Committee was forced to issue a press release. The joke seemed to be on the McCain campaign.

---

75   "McCain's Failed Facebook Satire", 25 August 2008, http://www.splicetoday.com/politics-and-media/mccain-s-failed-facebook-satire (accessed 23 June 2011).

4. Writing the tweets and posts that will come back to haunt you.

What campaigns often forget is that social media can be very unforgiving. What is sent out into the Twitterverse or on Facebook is set in stone. Posts, tweets, and other digital content are cyber immortal.

U.S. House Speaker Newt Gingrich learned this lesson when some of his tweets came back to haunt him. At first, he was a staunch supporter for pro-military action in Libya (and tweeted to that affect) and then later reversed his stance when Obama gave the green light to carry out airstrikes with NATO.[76] Being wishy-washy on twitter as in the political arena is a surefire way to get you noticed but it can cause voters to flip too.

During the 2010 presidential elections in the Philippines, candidate Benigno Aquino accidentally tweeted a personal rant on his official feed. "Won't be bringing a car to work! Stupid taxi who bumped my car! 5k down the drain!"[77] Although he went on to became the 15th President of the Philippines, the publicity was negative. As a candidate trying to win the hearts and minds of the people, his online complaining about a car dent didn't make him sound like a compassionate candidate or a man of the people.

---

76 "Elections 2012: The Social Network, Presidential Campaign Edition", 11 April 2011, http://www.huffingtonpost.com/2011/04/17/elections-2012-social-media_n_850172.html (accessed 23 June 2011).

77 "Noynoy Aquino Mistweet Message on Twitter", 23 March 2010, http://www.pinoysoundingboard.com/2010/03/noynoy-aquino-mistweet-message-on-twitter/ (accessed 19 June 2011).

5. Forgetting to engage supporters on their own terms; losing that authenticity.

One of the primary purposes of social networking sites is to create communities built on collaboration and interaction. As such, you must go beyond reposting and re-tweeting of information; adding your personal views, or referring to a comment made by one of your supporters. Ask a question.

One of the biggest mistakes campaigns make is slinking back into official-sounding mode once the campaign run is over. After winning a resounding victory at the polls in 2008, the Obama camp made the mistake of losing his momentum and interest in interacting with his constituents using social media.[78] Once in office, Obama toned down his tweets and posts. Many devolved into your typical press release-type sound bites, losing their authenticity:

"The small-business jobs bill passed today will provide loans and cut taxes for millions of small businesses without adding to our deficit."
"Making a personnel announcement this morning. Watch live at 11:05am ET."

78 "Obama's Post-Election Social Media Lapse", 29 October 2010, Fast Company, http://www.fastcompany.com/1698848/barack-obamas-post-election-social-media-lapse (accessed 20 June 2011).

A good example of a politician who has caught the public eye in his personal approach to social networking is Newark city Mayor Cory Booker. Reflecting his own approach to politics and engagement with the public, he said, "I'm always encouraging people to be mentors, to get involved in some substantive way…Democracy is not a spectator sport. Don't sit back on your tukhus and wait for change to happen. Get out there and make it happen. Whatever your passion is, get involved." [79]

6. Appearing too negative or critical.

Electoral politics is about winning— this means putting yourself in the best possible light relative to your opponent. However, there is a fine line between being competitive and bashing your political opponent, particularly on social media platforms. The effect can be annoying, distracting and demoralizing to supporters. Personal, day-to-day non-political rants of would-be officials should be closely monitored.

Scottish Labor Party candidate Stuart MacLennan committed Twitter suicide in 2010 when he posted a string of offensive rants and expletives on his Twitter page.[80] He had attacked Commons Speaker John Bercow, David Cameron, and Nick Clegg, the Liberal Democrat leader, among others. People were shocked and to contain the social media damage, the Labor Party dropped him as a candidate and suspended his membership to the party.

---

79   "Cory Brooker on Newark's Future: 'Watch Us Rise'", 22 March 2011, http://www.thedailybeast.com/articles/2011/03/22/newark-mayor-cory-booker-on-newarks-future-social-media-video-responses.html (accessed 19 June 2011).

80   "Labor Candidate Stuart MacLennan Sacked Over Twitter Rants", 9 April 2010, http://www.timesonline.co.uk/tol/news/politics/article7093061.ece (accessed 19 June 2011).

In the U.S., former House Speaker Newt Gingrich raised eyebrows when he expressed his disappointment at the Supreme Court appointment of Sonia Sotomayer, accusing her of being a "reverse racist".[81] On Twitter it generated heated debate when Gingrich wrote, "Imagine a judicial nominee said 'my experience as a white man makes me better than a Latina woman' new racism is no better than old racism." While many people appreciated his candor and strong views, it also made Gingrich appear defensive and combative.

7. Using inappropriate or off-putting video to make a point (it often backfires!)

Although former California Governor Arnold Schwarzenegger has a Hollywood pedigree, a political video that was meant to make a case for spending cuts— fell flat and put off a lot of people. In 2009, Schwarzenegger made a video of himself holding up a big knife while making a speech about the importance of cutting state costs in California.[82] It was meant to be bold and visually-arresting, but the video reeked of gimmickry.

8. TMI – Too much information

Michigan's 2nd District Congressman Peter Hoekstra invited criticism during a trip to Iraq in 2009 when he gave detailed information

---

81   "Newt Gingrich on Twitter: Sonia Sotomayor 'Racist', Should Withdraw", 27 May 2009, http://abcnews.go.com/Politics/SoniaSotomayor/story?id=7685284 (accessed 23 June 2011)

82   "Why is Arnold Schwarzenegger Brandishing a Gigantic Knife?", 22 July 2009, http://www.huffingtonpost.com/2009/07/22/why-is-arnold-schwarzeneg_n_242964.html (accessed 19 June 2011).

regarding his itinerary and trip on Twitter.[83] Hoekstra defended himself and said that other officials have broadcast their schedules on Twitter. However, the Pentagon didn't take the issue lightly and has gone on to review its policy. On the matters of national security, it's understandable to keep mission-related information under wraps.

Missouri U.S. Senator Claire McCaskill put off some of her constituents when she tweeted, "Tired of looking and feeling fat. Maybe talking about it publicly will keep me on track as I try to be more disciplined. Off to the gym."[84] Although such statements aren't controversial, coming from a public figure it can raise some eyebrows and call into question the appropriateness of blurring the boundaries between professional and personal life.

9. Lack of discretion in sharing information.

In 2009, unable to contain his excitement on the possible shifting of power in the Virginia state senate to the Republicans, Republican Party Chairman of Virginia tweeted about a possible defection of one of the Democrats, Ralph Northam.[85] Of course the Democrats got a wind of the tweet, and made sure that Northam stayed put in the party. Democrats held control of the state legislature 21-19.

---

83   "Congressman Peter Hoekstra Twitters His Secret Iraqi Trip", 9 February 2009, http://www.associatedcontent.com/article/1460684/congressman_peter_hoekstra_ twitters.html (accessed 20 June 2011)

84   "Quotes", http://newsfeed.time.com/2011/05/12/quote-sen-claire-mccaskill-tweets-that-she-feels-fat/ (accessed 25 June 2011).

85   "Jeff Frederick's Twitter Use Foils GOP Virginia Senate Coup", 10 February 2009, The Huffington Post, http://www.huffingtonpost.com/2009/02/10/jeff-fredericks-twitter-u_n_165769.html (accessed 19 June 2011).

10. Lack of basic decency and social decorum.

Social decorum doesn't end when you're sitting in front of your computer, your persona hidden. Best to keep your pants on when using social media sites to avoid the temptation to be adventurous and inappropriate— especially if you're a politician and in a position to become New York City's next mayor. New York Democratic Representative Anthony Weiner was forced to resign after tweeting a lewd photo of himself in boxer shorts to a college student, Gennette Cordova.[86] Soon after, a slew of photos were circulated on the web. The very public humiliation cost him his career and his seat in Congress.

---

86 "Weiner Resign in Chaotic Final Scene", 16 June 2011, The New York Times, http://www.nytimes.com/2011/06/17/nyregion/anthony-d-weiner-tells-friends-he-will-resign.html?_r=1 (accessed 19 June 2011).

Chapter 6

Socially Tactical Strategies

BEYOND ENGAGING in social networks and building up a social media presence, effective campaigns should also examine how they can use social media in a more tactical manner, keeping in mind the opposition. Social media is a double-edged sword which can be used to offensively and defensively.

There are several reasons why political campaigns should look to social media as a central foundation of their efforts:

1. Social media has traction and staying power.

Any reviews, comments, blogs and videos supporting or attacking your campaign stick around for a very long time— becoming the equivalent of permanent marker on the new paintjob. Remember, content can stay afloat on the web long after the initial buzz, only to be resurrected later to the benefit or detriment of the campaign.

2. Social media is mobile and spreads quickly.

Blogs, videos, Facebook posts, and tweets are shared and passed around the Web through social networks. Not only can content be replicated, it can also be modified. Running commentary on a Facebook post or blog can be copied and pasted, misquoted, and altered. A polite disagreement on your Facebook page over a campaign post can escalate in tone and intensity as communication is passed around.

3. Social media is a catalyst.

Othman Laraki, the Director of Search and Geo at Twitter, once called Twitter an integral part of a revolution equation, "reducing the cost of dissent and [increasing] the cost of suppressing it".[87] Obama's 2008 presidential campaign showed that ordinary citizens could collectively organize. Access to social media provides the necessary spark.

---

87 "Economics of dissent: How Twitter and Facebook tipped the revolutionary equation", 17 March 2011, CNN Money, http://tech.fortune.cnn.com/2011/03/17/economics-of-dissent-how-twitter-and-facebook-tipped-the-revolutionary-equation/ (accessed 29 June 2011).

Reputation Management through Social Media and ORM

Social Branding: How to Tailor Your Digital Profiles to Build Loyalty

Why Does Branding Matter?

Branding, in relation to political marketing, "is what [a politician] stands for and what [he or she] is known for." It's not direct mail, design, or advertising; it's something that happens well before any of those elements of marketing take place.[88] A politician's brand— and the consistent use and application of that brand— is vital to a candidate's success. A poorly defined brand can cause every other element of a political campaign to suffer.

If websites are the most important secondary "interaction" a voter has with a politician, then branding is perhaps the most important element of a political campaign, period. While most people think that branding and marketing are interchangeable terms, experts beg to differ. Branding, rather, is something that should occur before a marketing campaign ever begins. It is a politician's "personality"— everything that he or she believes in, represents, and hopes to accomplish. Moreover, a brand is a "promise [made] to the world."[89] In addition to defining a mission, a campaign's brand strategy also gives guidelines for elements like de-

---

88   "A Practical Guide to Branding", Bloomberg Business Week, http://www.businessweek.com/smallbiz/content/jun2008/sb2008069_694225.htm (accessed 22 June 2011).

89   "A Practical Guide to Branding", Bloomberg Business Week, http://www.businessweek.com/smallbiz/content/jun2008/sb2008069_694225.htm (accessed 22 June 2011).

sign, color scheme, and content. A political campaign has much to gain from clearly defining the candidate's brand from the outset, then using it as a guide for all public interaction, marketing, or communication. With so much being communicated in a politician's brand, executing good branding is crucial to a successful election.

Essential Principles of Branding for Political Campaigns

While there are many principles of web design and branding, eight stand out as most important to a political campaign. Below, each of these principles is discussed in depth.

1. Be unique and easy to recognize.

The brand, the essence of a campaign or candidate, should be easy to differentiate from the competition and applied consistently. All marketing materials— the website, print materials, television and radio commercials, Facebook, and Twitter, among others— should work together to reinforce the politician's purpose, goal, and message. Social media should work hand-in-hand with the website to reinforce the brand, ensuring that the entire campaign is cohesive, consistent, and well-executed.

A successful campaign site should also be different, distinct, and call attention to the uniqueness of that particular candidate. Flags and stars have been done and red, white, and blue sometimes seem to be the only colors available in a political website designer's palette. Of course, these elements can be used, but the trick is finding a new and interesting way to use them.

In a survey of the top five Senator websites, the *Bivings Report* praised things like, "confidence in the design," a "palette [that] is unique for a political site," and being "totally different (at first glance)".[90] By creating a clear and consistent brand that is different and unique, and then consistently applying that brand to all marketing and media, a candidate will surely stand out from the competition. And, by differentiating from other campaigns, candidates are more likely to be remembered…and voted for.

2. Clearly define the brand and establish guidelines and rules on design elements and messaging.

Good brand strategy includes a guidebook or stylebook that clearly defines the brand, including specific design elements (logo, color palette, etc.), written content (tagline, mission statement, etc.), and a variety of other elements that make up the brand. These guidelines should also include usage rules (e.g. "the logo should never be printed larger than 6 inches by 6 inches" or "the word 'Southerner,' should not be used in any online or print content"). The clearer the guidelines, the less room there is for mistakes.

3. Utilize space effectively.

Before all other elements of website design come into play, a website must have proper utilization of screen space. In web design, a website's "prime real estate" lies above the "fold", which is an area "viewable without further action".[91] According to Jakob Nielsen, one of the fore-

---

90   "Top 5 Best Senate Campaign Website Designs", The Bivings Report, http://www.bivingsreport.com/2008/top-5-senate-campaign-website-designs/ (accessed 22 June 2011).

91   "Scrolling and Attention," Jakob Nielsen's Alert Box, http://www.useit.com/alertbox/scrolling-attention.html (accessed 25 June 2011).

most experts on web usability, "the most salient information [should be] within a page's initially viewable area".[92] Most websites, however, use less than half of the space available to them, trying to cram a lot of content into a small area and wasting a great deal of screen space.[93] He further explains that the eye-tracking area on a website typically favors the top portion of the page (above the fold), where 80.3 percent of users' time with a particular website is spent.[94] Furthermore, eye tracking tends to go from left to right, with 69 percent of viewing time on the left side of the screen.[95] Despite the available information, many websites fail to capitalize on this precious space, causing user frustration and, often, losing them for good in the process.

4. Usability is key.

More than 83 percent of website users will leave a site after two clicks if the information he or she is looking for can't be found. Furthermore, studies have shown that viewers have certain expectations when they visit a site; they expect a heading or title at the top, navigation along the left side or top, and "small print (i.e. terms of use [and] privacy)" along the bottom.[96] Keeping this in mind, user-friendly navigation, well-placed content, and a clear call to action— above the fold and within

---

92   "Scrolling and Attention," Jakob Nielsen's Alert Box, http://www.useit.com/alert-box/scrolling-attention.html (accessed 25 June 2011).

93   "Scrolling and Attention," Jakob Nielsen's Alert Box, http://www.useit.com/alert-box/scrolling-attention.html (accessed 25 June 2011).

94   "Scrolling and Attention," Jakob Nielsen's Alert Box, http://www.useit.com/alert-box/scrolling-attention.html (accessed 25 June 2011).

95   "Scrolling and Attention," Jakob Nielsen's Alert Box, http://www.useit.com/alert-box/scrolling-attention.html (accessed 25 June 2011).

96   "Political Web Design", Political Web Marketing, http://www.politicalwebmarket-ing.com/political-website-design.php (accessed 25 June 2011).

the eye tracking area— is vital to a successful website. By fulfilling a viewer's (and potential voter's) expectations, he or she is much more likely to stay on the site and learn about the political campaign.

Furthermore, considering that a good website fully utilizes the eye tracking area with the most pertinent content above the fold, political websites should pay particular attention to where the call to action is placed. Along with a clear campaign message, a bold, prominent call to action, such as "Join the Campaign," "Volunteer," or "Donate to the Cause," should catch a viewer's eye.[97]

5. Don't lose viewers at the homepage.

According to Jakob Nielsen, a website's homepage has two main purposes: to provide users with information and "to serve as [a] top-level navigation for information that's inside the site." A homepage's third purpose is to communicate the website's purpose, which can be done through a logo and tagline. In a survey of 50 websites, content and navigation accounted for a shockingly small 39 percent of usable screen space. [98]

So, how can a political homepage attract and retain visitors? Nielsen offers several suggestions, which will be adapted here to reflect the specific needs of a campaign site. First, the homepage must have a memorable and distinct look, which users instantly recognize when navigating back to it. Second, a politician's name, logo, and a tagline that "explicitly summarizes what a [politician] does" should be prominently placed

---

97   "Top 5 Best Senate Campaign Website Designs", The Bivings Report, http://www.bivingsreport.com/2008/top-5-senate-campaign-website-designs/ (accessed 22 June 2011).

98   "Homepage Real Estate Allocation", Jakob Nielsen's Alert Box, http://www.useit.com/alertbox/20030210.html (accessed 25 June 2011).

and large enough to be easily noticeable. Third, high-priority tasks, information, or call-outs should be emphasized. These elements should be displayed prominently, preferably in the upper-middle portion of the screen; furthermore, this information should be kept simple with about one to four tasks or call-outs.[99] While Nielsen offers many other suggestions, implementing these three will greatly enhance a campaign's site.

6. Be visually pleasing.

In taking all of the important elements of a strategically created brand and well-designed website, don't forget that it needs to be pretty. Websites should be pleasing to the eye— taking into account the rules of design (rule of thirds, balance, emphasis, etc.)— use white space effectively, and not be over designed. Essentially, content should not be crammed, there should be ample (but not too much) space between the elements on the page, important elements should be bold and catch a viewer's attention, and the rule of KISS (Keep It Simple Stupid) should be applied. That is, the simplest design, content, and layout should be used—there is no need to complicate things with fancy graphics or unnecessary content.[100] The simpler and more straightforward a site is, the more likely a visitor is to fully understand the candidate's purpose and mission.

7. Consider the audience.

A politician's brand, as well as website design and content, should always keep the audience in consideration. Using voter-focused lan-

---

99   "113 Design Guidelines for Homepage Usability," Jakob Nielsen's Alert Box, http://www.useit.com/homepageusability/guidelines.html (accessed 25 June 2011).

100   "KISS Basic Web Design Principles", Deep Web Web Design, http://www.deep-web.co.nz/KISS-basic-web-design.php (accessed 25 June 2011).

guage in call-outs, content, and navigation elements will help align the site with the values of the voter, rather than the candidate.[101] (A brand strategy that has a voter-centered focus can help keep this in check.) A candidate's mission statement should be easily recognizable and consistently communicated throughout the entirety of the site, enhancing credibility and consistency, as well as properly communicating the focus of the campaign. And, since "credibility is fast becoming a key usability issue," a website should include "Contact Us" and "About Us" pages, which at least includes a phone number, e-mail, or mailing address.[102]

8. Be politically minded.

Remember, not all websites are created equal. Effective campaign sites have certain page elements that can (and must) be included for it to be fully effective, reach viewers, and further campaign goals. In addition to the elements discussed above, a campaign site should be search engine friendly and, since most visitors will only wait about seven seconds for a page to load, quick to download.[103] Also, a good campaign site should include links to the candidate's social media accounts.

Perhaps more importantly, however, is a willingness to evaluate a website's effectiveness and change the elements that aren't working. Think of a website as an organic, ever-evolving campaign element; it's not "done" after it goes live. Regularly updated content will keep

---

101   "113 Design Guidelines for Homepage Usability", Jakob Nielsen's Alert Box, http://www.useit.com/homepageusability/guidelines.html (accessed 25 June 2011).

102   "Political Web Design", Political Web Marketing, https://www.scrible.com/contentview/archive/page/AGO2091HIK5OPJ3A30O1G3BACKC4K603/index.html (accessed 25 June 2011).

103   "Political Web Design", Political Web Marketing, https://www.scrible.com/contentview/archive/page/AGO2091HIK5OPJ3A30O1G3BACKC4K603/index.html (accessed 25 June 2011).

visitors (potential voters) coming back to read the latest news, ideas, or updates. And, while expert opinion is helpful, getting feedback from everyday, average users is key to ensuring that the site is meeting the needs of the intended audience.[104] If it isn't, be sure to fix the things that aren't working. Remember, a website essentially is the candidate—thus, it's important to continually evaluate and revise the site's content and design.

Examples of Campaigns that Build 'Brand'

While there are many examples of good campaign sites (and exponentially more bad examples), a few stand out for the purposes of this analysis. Drawing upon the *Bivings Report*'s "Top Five Best Senate Website Designs" and *OhMyGov*'s "Best Campaign Websites in 2010: The Governors," we will look at three sites that use many of the principles of good design and branding. Both the *Bivings Report* and *OhMyGov* conducted well-executed surveys, taking into account several of the aforementioned design and branding principles.

Case Study 1: Gordon Smith, 2008 Senate candidate

Of particular interest is the 2008 Senate candidate Gordon Smith's website.[105] In regards to brand differentiation, Smith's site (and, therefore, Smith himself) can be considered a prime example for establishing a feel that is refreshingly different. Although the site doesn't fully utilize the "prime

---

104   "Political Web Design", Political Web Marketing, https://www.scrible.com/contentview/archive/page/AGO2091HIK5OPJ3A3OO1G3BACKC4K603/index.html (accessed 25 June 2011).

105   "Top 5 Best Senate Campaign Website Designs", The Bivings Report, http://www.bivingsreport.com/2008/top-5-senate-campaign-website-designs/ (accessed 22 June 2011).

real estate" available on the homepage, it does apply the KISS principle of simple, clean design and copy. As the *Bivings Report* notes, there is one news item and one call-out, saving the viewer from the cluttered array of information present on many others candidates' sites. Furthermore, the website puts extreme emphasis on the audience— Oregon voters— by including a large, beautiful landscape photo. The navigation is where it is expected to be, at the top of the page. Furthermore, the donation link is understated, subtly communicating that the number-one priority isn't money. All in all, this non-traditional site aptly applies many of the principles of design and branding, with a unique twist.

Case Study 2: Mike Cox, 2010 gubernatorial candidate

While Mike Cox's 2010 gubernatorial campaign site doesn't utilize the fold properly, it does do a lot of things right.[106] According to *OhMyGov*, Cox's site was a "'call to action' champion, featuring a Volunteer of the Week and laying out a compelling 4-step process on the homepage of how supporters could help the campaign". The very top of the page includes links to Facebook, LinkedIn, Twitter, Flickr, and You-Tube, which are set above the main navigation items. The site does an especially effective job of using voter language by naming the navigation items, "Meet Mike", "Why I Am Running", and "My Plan." The site also utilizes white space effectively, although it does not fully utilize the eye tracking area. While the colors are typical, the design is bold and eye-catching, making it stand out from the typical candidate website. All in all, it was a well-executed site that utilized many of the principles of design.

---

106 "Best Campaign Websites in 2010: The Governors", OhMyGovNews, http://ohmygov.com/blogs/general_news/archive/2010/08/05/Best-Campaign-Websites-in-2010-The-Governors.aspx (accessed 25 June 2011).

Both of these sites, along with other best-practice sites, do something similar: they capitalize on mini-campaigns that appeal to different voter constituencies. While these mini-campaigns all target different issues and audiences, they work together to form a unified whole and consistent vision, reflecting on the candidate's brand.

Case Study 3: Scott Kleeb, 2008 Senate candidate

Scott Kleeb's website, which was rated the number one 2008 Senate Campaign Site by the Bivings Report, fully utilizes this idea of breaking the larger campaign into smaller, targeted issues.[107] In addition to an incredibly well-designed homepage, a very unique 'ranch-focused' brand, and the use of several elements of design, Kleeb's campaign also breaks its mission into several, different missions or issues, thereby appealing to several types of voters. These include, "Leading by Listening in Bellevue," "Nebraska's Brand of Change," and "The Building a Better Alaska Tour". Furthermore, the most prominent text reads, "Become a Ranch Hand Volunteer"— something you won't find on most political websites. While these issues appeal to different voters, they also relate to the campaign's mission and brand, making Kleeb's site an apt example of great campaign website design.

---

107   "Top 5 Best Senate Campaign Website Designs", The Bivings Report, http://www.bivingsreport.com/2008/top-5-senate-campaign-website-designs/ (accessed 22 June 2011).

Got Digital Weak Spots?

Practicing Online Reputation Management (ORM)

While a politician's website is important, it's certainly not the only 'interaction' that potential voters will have with a campaign. The creation of a brand, and consistent application of that brand, must extend to social media sites as well. But, even the most well-intentioned campaign and thoroughly-thought brand can go horribly wrong when faced with digital weak spots like embarrassing photos, contradictory statements, or negative associations.

To avoid the painful process of damage control after the fact, well-planned online reputation management (ORM) must be implemented—before a problem occurs.[108]

Establish a Socially Tactical Social Media Policy

Although the exact definition of the term "Web 2.0" is debatable, the facts are not: today's Internet framework makes all web-based information potentially permanent.[109] And, while the tone of social media venues like Facebook and Twitter may tend to be a bit more personal and less formal than web content, radio, and television, it must also meet certain standards. By writing and enforcing a social media policy, campaigns can avoid damaging content, embarrassing information or photos, and regrettably bad status updates.

---

108 Agranoff, Craig and Tabin, Herb, 2010, Do It Yourself Online Reputation Management: A Step-By-Step Guide To Building Or Repairing Your Online Reputation (Pendant Publishing).

109 "How To Develop a Social Media Policy and Protect Your Company's Reputation." Reputation.com, http://www.reputation.com/how_to/develop-social-media-policy-and-protect-reputation/ (accessed 26 June 2011).

According to Reputation.com, a company that specializes in online reputation management, a robust and effective "social media policy expands beyond the workplace, providing a framework for both personal and professional social media conduct."[110] By taking proactive, rather than reactive, steps toward combating any number of social media *faux pas*, politicians can work toward building their brand, mission, and purpose— rather than recovering from a bad reputation.

Reputation.com suggests that social media policy should:[111]

- **Specify how campaign members and politicians can use both campaign-related and personal social media sites (personal blogs, Twitter, YouTube, Facebook, etc.);**

- **Establish that the individual is responsible for all material posted; and**

- **Ensure that no negative (or possibly negative) information should be posted about the campaign.**

Furthermore, all information posted online should be honest and accurate, and a campaign member should always respect confidentiality. The policy should not only list what a member or politician can't do, but what he or she can do as well; and, the policy should be reviewed by an attorney that is well-versed in this arena.[112]

---

110 "How To Develop a Social Media Policy and Protect Your Company's Reputation." Reputation.com, http://www.reputation.com/how_to/develop-social-media-policy-and-protect-reputation/ (accessed 26 June 2011).

111 Reputation.com's suggestions have been modified here to fit the specific needs of political campaigns.

112 "How To Develop a Social Media Policy and Protect Your Company's Reputation." Reputation.com, http://www.reputation.com/how_to/develop-social-media-policy-

Use Sentiment Analysis in Twitterverse

With all of the various online venues that positive or negative content can occur, how can one possibly monitor it all?

Sentiment analysis, which is by no means a be-all and end-all, can help in analyzing what people in "Twitterverse" are saying about a particular politician. Through sentiment analysis, which is available through a number of both computer and human evaluated services, the percentage of positive and negative sentiment toward a term (e.g. "Obama") can be loosely quantified. It determines shifts in public opinion by analyzing the language in the content of tweets on Twitter and other online 'conversations'. Campaigns can use this data to determine quickly which messages are resonating with potential voters, and which messages are falling flat. By evaluating "tweets" on Twitter, this automated software determines the feeling or emotion (sentiment) of posted content, giving it a positive or negative rating. For large campaigns, automated sentiment can be a useful tool in determining the public's feeling toward a candidate or issue.[113]

Of the many sites available to analyze sentiment in Twitterverse, notable services include Twitter Sentiment, TweetFeel, and TweetTone, among others.[114]

To analyze the sentiment surrounding a word or name, simply type it into the search field on the site's homepage. It's important to note that all sentiment analysis software works differently and categorizes

---

and-protect-reputation/ (accessed 26 June 2011).

113 "How Companies Can Use Sentiment Analysis to Improve Their Business", Mashable.com, http://mashable.com/2010/04/19/sentiment-analysis/ (accessed 26 June 2011).

114 "Sentiment Analysis Sites", Twitter Sentiment, https://sites.google.com/site/twittersentimenthelp/other-resources (accessed 27 June 2011).

things in different fashions—leading, of course, to discrepancies. For example, while Twitter Sentiment categorizes sentiment by "the good and the bad," TweetTone breaks tweets up into more distinct categories like, "Friendly," "Content," "Uneasy," and "Shame".

Furthermore, to highlight the drastic differences between the sites, typing the same term, "Obama," leads to incredibly varied results. While Twitter Sentiment instantly comes up with over 400,000 results (93 percent of which are negative), TweetFeel has a constantly updated stream of tweets that gives an average sentiment rating (50 to 60 percent, depending on the moment). Clearly, sentiment analysis is a good starting point, but must be supplemented with thorough, preemptive ORM.

Dig up the Dirt on Yourself—Before your Opponents Do

User-generated content means that anyone can write anything they want about a candidate, instantaneously— whether it's true or not. Rumors can spread within a matter of seconds, especially if they are controversial in nature. Remember, ORM "is not just about managing what you say but also about managing what others say as well."[115]

Once embarrassing photos, contradictory (or false) statements, or previous associations (such as, in Obama's case, the false connection to a radical religious group) are online, it's nearly impossible to get them to "go away". In fact, the effects of negative press can be so devastating that some companies are now paying as much as $5 million annually for $100 million brand restoration insurance, which helps restore a brand that has fallen victim to bad press, social media, and the like.[116]

---

115   "Online Reputation Management: Fact or Fiction?", http://www.barrywheeler.ca/online-reputation-management-fact-or-fiction/ (accessed 26 June 2011).

116   "Corporate Emergencies Now Call on Brand Restoration Insurance", Online Reputation Management, http://www.onlinerepmanagement.com/2011/06/corporate-emergencies-now-call-on-brand-restoration-insurance.html (accessed 26 June 2011).

Even if you delete and scrub clean incriminating photos from your blog, website, or Facebook page, it can still live on if people have caught wind of it, taking screen shots or re-posting a quote or photo somewhere else. What a candidate did in college five years ago— can come back and haunt him or her.

Case Study: ORM Gone Wrong

We don't often hear of the things avoided by quick-acting ORM, but we regularly hear, read, and talk about campaigns and politicians being destroyed because of deep web searches, a hacked Facebook account, or a poorly worded tweet. Such was the case in Representative Anthony Weiner's situation, although none of the above happened— he accidentally tweeted an inappropriate photo on his Twitter account, @RepWeiner. And, of course, the backlash was predictable: Twitterverse, bloggers, major news networks, and practically all of America knew about it in a matter of minutes and hours. Andrew Breitbart's blog, Big Government, first exposed the truth behind the photo, claiming that Weiner was having an inappropriate Internet relationship.[117] Deep web searches by ABC led to finding even more condemning photos of Weiner, which had apparently been uploaded by Weiner to an online site meant to hide photos; apparently, the site didn't do its job well enough.[118] After trying all of the typical tactics— denial, blaming a hacker, refusing to admit guilt— he finally admitted, "The picture

---

117 "Weinergate Bombshell: New Woman Comes Forward Claiming Cache of Intimate Photos and Online Communications with Beleaguered Congressman", http://biggovernment.com/abreitbart/2011/06/06/weinergate-bombshell-new-woman-comes-forward-claiming-cache-of-intimate-photos-and-online-communications-with-beleaguered-congressman/ (accessed 27 June 2011).

118 "Rep. Anthony Weiner: 'The Picture Was of Me and I Sent It'", ABC News Politics, http://abcnews.go.com/Politics/rep-anthony-weiner-picture/story?id=13774605 (accessed 27 June 2011).

was of me, and I sent it."[119]

Social media, as highlighted by Weiner's case, can kill a politician's reputation. According to a sentiment analysis from Gregory FCA, prior to his inappropriate tweet, Weiner rated 4.1 out of 5; from May 26th to June 7th, 2011, he dropped to a -2.[120] Analysts believe that much of this was due to denial of the act, although it's difficult to predict how the public would have reacted if he had told the truth.

Good ORM, a proactive social media team, and good common sense could have easily avoided this issue. As it stands, however, those images will be available in visible and deep web searches for the rest of his political and personal life.

Conduct Deep Web Searches

To add to the complexities of building, maintaining, and protecting an online presence, the Internet contains two layers: the "visible web" and "invisible web". General web searches using search engines like Google or Yahoo give results from the visible web. The invisible web— or, the "deep web"— is a bit more difficult to navigate.[121] The deep web contains content that is not part of the surface web, which is indexed by standard search engines. In fact, most of the web's information is buried far down on dynamically generated sites, in online databases that

---

119   "Rep. Anthony Weiner: 'The Picture Was of Me and I Sent It'", ABC News Politics, http://abcnews.go.com/Politics/rep-anthony-weiner-picture/story?id=13774605 (accessed 27 June 2011).

120   "What Anthony Weiner can teach us about online reputation management", http://blog.gregoryfca.com/2011/06/what-anthony-weiner-can-teach-us-about.html (accessed 27 June 2011),

121   "Invisible Web: What it is, Why it exists, How to find it, and Its inherent ambiguity", UC Berkeley Teaching Library Internet Workshops, http://www.lib.berkeley.edu/TeachingLib/Guides/Internet/InvisibleWeb.html (accessed 26 June 2011).

general-purpose web crawlers cannot reach.[122] And, it can contain a vast amount of information that goes years, even decades, back and could potentially ruin a candidate's campaign.

Real-time and deep web searches allow people (and potential voters) access to nearly every piece of available online information about a politician or campaign. This includes photos, status updates, blogs, YouTube videos, and a variety of other social media sources that are "wild" and loosely monitored.[123]

1. Conduct a "vanity search" using deep search engines.

There are several web resources that any campaign can utilize for free, including KGBPeople.com, Yasni.com, PIPL.com, and PeekYou. com. Other deep search engines include Spokeo.com, 123people. com, Wink.com, Rapleaf.com, Zabasearch.com, WhoIsHim.com, and iSearch.com.

2. Use ultra-deep, paid services for more thorough checks.

While the Internet provides a lot of information for free, private databases exist that can offer much more information for political campaigns. These pay-for-services cannot be altered like the Internet. One example of these premium services is Intelius. Intelius is an online public records company, offering a variety of services to both consumers

---

122   Agranoff, Craig and Tabin, Herb, 2010, Do It Yourself Online Reputation Management: A Step-By-Step Guide To Building Or Repairing Your Online Reputation (Pendant Publishing).

123   "Online Reputation Management: Fact or Fiction?", Barry Wheeler, http://www. barrywheeler.ca/online-reputation-management-fact-or-fiction/ (accessed 26 June 2011).

and businesses, including civil and criminal records. Known primarily for its background search service, Intelius, is at the forefront of providing background searches on individuals.

For $39.95, Intelius will do a background search of public records and provide information on virtually anyone. In addition to background checks, Intelius markets its services to landlords, employers, and other businesses. By also providing credit checks, criminal and sex offender checks, and reverse phone directory services, Intelius utilizes its valuable database to provide many types of information— at a price. However, Intelius also has some free services: "People Search" and "Email Search". Also, you can obtain limited information by entering a social security number, cellular phone number, or address. Intelius also offers an iPhone app that lets you run a criminal record and background check right on your phone. Just enter a name or cell phone number to search publicly available records. It even features a 'Sleaze Detector', which scans criminal records to determine if anyone with that name has been charged with drug possession, assault and battery, sex crimes, DUI, and other offenses.

Take Proactive Measures

Since this insurance isn't available to politicians just yet, there are a few tactics that can be employed to counteract the negative impact bad press can have on a campaign:

1. Move quickly.

The faster a campaign responds to negative content, the quicker it can be counteracted and, hopefully, resolved. The longer the content is allowed to circulate cyberspace without a response, the deeper it becomes entrenched in the visible and deep web, making it nearly impossible to get rid of.[124]

2. Keep content fresh and positive through comments.

Most social media venues allow users to post a response or comment. Clarifying or counteracting a negative video, status update, news article, blog post, or similar form of bad press can help placate the situation (although it won't delete the negative content). However, this can backfire: keeping the conversation going keeps the content fresh, both on the site and in search engines.[125]

3. Flood the web with positive content.

Posting positive content about a campaign or politician can drive that content to the top results of searches and help generate more traffic to a campaign site, Facebook page, or Twitter feed, rather than to a negative blog or article about the candidate.[126] This content must be prolific and generate viewer response, however, or it will not serve its purpose.

---

124 "Online Reputation Management: Fact or Fiction?", Barry Wheeler, http://www.barrywheeler.ca/online-reputation-management-fact-or-fiction/ (accessed 26 June 2011).

125 "Online Reputation Management: Fact or Fiction?", Barry Wheeler, http://www.barrywheeler.ca/online-reputation-management-fact-or-fiction/ (accessed 26 June 2011).

126 "Online Reputation Management: Fact or Fiction?", Barry Wheeler, http://www.barrywheeler.ca/online-reputation-management-fact-or-fiction/ (accessed 26 June 2011).

4. Use search engine optimization (SEO).

Optimizing a website's or blog's code and content can help drive more viewers to the site and, therefore, less traffic to sites with negative information or content.

5. Ask nicely.

As a last resort, ask websites to remove the content. Some websites, when asked, will oblige; Google will not do this, however.[127]

6. Invest in ORM.

Online reputation management needs a budget, just like any other part of a political campaign. A politician's web presence should be constantly monitored, daily and hourly, to avoid scandal. Allocating a portion of the budget to this can do a great deal of good for a campaign.[128]

---

127   "Online Reputation Management: Fact or Fiction?", Barry Wheeler, http://www.barrywheeler.ca/online-reputation-management-fact-or-fiction/ (accessed 26 June 2011).

128   "Online Reputation Management: Fact or Fiction?", Barry Wheeler, http://www.barrywheeler.ca/online-reputation-management-fact-or-fiction/ (accessed 26 June 2011).

Engaging the Opposition

Larry Zilliox, private investigator for Investigative Research Specialists and author of *Opposition Research Handbook: A Guide To Political Investigations*, has compared opposition research in political campaigns to espionage. "Really it's about public records, interviewing, finding information, tracking the spoken word," he said.[129] Opposition research has always been a part of the political landscape. Lately, access has moved to the digital realm.

During the 2008 presidential elections, opposition researchers for McCain and Obama trawled the web for incriminating or inflammatory evidence. Opposition researchers cast suspicion on Obama's supposed Muslim roots and found videos of McCain boasting that he was fine with U.S. occupation of Iraq lasting 100 years.

In an article published by the Center for Public Integrity, researchers found that opposition research has become part of the business of doing politics:[130]

---

129   "Opposition Research: Facebook Tried To Play The Politics Game", 16 May 2011, http://turnstylenews.com/2011/05/16/opposition-research-facebook-tried-to-play-the-politics-game/ (accessed 29 June 2011).

130   "The Buying of the President 2008", 30 May 2008, The Center for Public Integrity, http://www.buyingofthepresident.org/index.php/stories/dirty_politics/ (accessed 29 June 2011).

"In any presidential campaign, successful candidates have two fairly simple imperatives. The first is relatively easy: to promote yourself. The other is to knock down your opponent. This side of the equation can get nasty — smears, misleading advertising, and outright dirty tricks make up the dark underbelly of the democratic process. The political operatives whose specialty this is, known as opposition researchers, are widely considered the lowest form of life in the campaign business. Their work happens below the radar screen and outside the polite forums of televised debates and Iowa barbeque cook-offs. It's also what usually makes or breaks a candidate for the White House."

In the age of Facebook and Twitter, opposition research is now much easier. Social media platforms can be a boom and a bane to every political campaign. For example, Facebook photos are often the weapons of choice among opposition researchers. In 2009, during a 32nd Congressional District special election to replace Hilda Solis, frontrunner Democrat Gil Cedillo distributed posters aimed at discrediting contender, Emanuel Pleitez. The photos showed Pleitez at parties drinking alcohol and socializing with alleged gang members. A few photos showed him flashing gang signs with his hands.[131] Neither Pleitez nor Cedillo won the election, but it reflected the power of social media in becoming a rich information source for political opponents. As one opposition researcher put it, "Most times you have to get someone's enemies to give you an embarrassing photo. Now, candidates themselves are posting them on the Internet."

---

131   "Young Political Candidates Confronted by Digital Past", 17 November 2009, PBS Media Shift, http://www.pbs.org/mediashift/2009/11/young-political-candidates-confronted-by-digital-past-on-facebook321.html (accessed 29 June 2011).

Stay on the Offensive

It's been said that one damaging blog post is worth more than $100,000 spent on a "mudslinging" ad.[132] And, with the speed that untruths can spread on the Internet, that statement is very likely true. Unfortunately, a pervasive enough rumor can attach itself to a politician's campaign, and the stain it leaves is very hard to remove. So, what's a politician to do in these cases? How can one combat damaging rumors? Good ORM, a quick response, and honesty can go far in combating political smears.

Political smear campaigns are likely one of the most feared events that can occur in a politician's career. Political smears are "widely distributed negative labels intended to slander a prominent political figure." Unfortunately, a widely accepted smear— no matter how ridiculously untrue it may be— can cost a great deal in damage control. Even worse, they have "the unsavory consequence of instilling implicit cognitive associations consistent with smear attacks in the minds of citizens."[133] Thus, if a smear campaign is widespread enough, especially in a candidate's early stages of campaigning, it may become nearly impossible to separate the association between the candidate and the untrue smear.

Although political smears have been around since the late 1700s, the most recent grand scale smears to reach American voters were during the 2008 presidential elections. At one point, Obama was called a

---

132   "The $100,000 Blog Post – Politics' New Make or Break Media", Online Reputation Management, http://www.onlinerepmanagement.com/2006/10/the-100000-blog-post-politics-new-make-or-break-media.html (accessed 27 June 2011).

133   "Smearing the Opposition: Implicit and Explicit Stigmatization of the 2008 U.S. Presidential Candidates and the Current U.S. President." Journal of Experimental Psychology, http://news.msu.edu/media/documents/2010/08/a8099abf-c5dd-439f-95d5-64178e629848.pdf (accessed 27 June 2011).

Muslim extremist, while McCain was said to be diagnosed as senile. Of course, neither of these statements is true.[134]

Just how pervasive are these smears? In a psychological study, participants were flashed photos of both Obama and McCain, separately. The flash was so quick that they could not distinguish the subjects in the photos. Nonetheless, McCain supporters who were flashed Obama's photo thought of words like, "Arab, turban, and mosque". Likewise, Obama supporters who were flashed McCain's photo thought of words like, "senile, dementia, and Alzheimer's". These associations were so innate and unconscious that they were felt and thought, without consciously recognizing the photos. The same thing did not happen when flashed a photo of the candidate they supported. The study further found that reminding participants of their race, age, and party affiliation made them more likely to accept false information about a candidate. It's this "us" and "them" mentality that causes the public to accept even the most outlandish rumors.[135]

---

134   "Smearing the Opposition: Implicit and Explicit Stigmatization of the 2008 U.S. Presidential Candidates and the Current U.S. President." Journal of Experimental Psychology, http://news.msu.edu/media/documents/2010/08/a8099abf-c5dd-439f-95d5-64178e629848.pdf (accessed 27 June 2011).

135   "Senile McCain, Extremist Obama", Psychology Today, http://www.psychology-today.com/blog/the-hidden-brain/201010/senile-mccain-extremist-obama (accessed 27 June 2011).

Debunk False Rumors and Smears

A good ORM program engages the opposition, rather than waiting for further attack. In doing so, it takes a proactive approach to a situation that could turn out to be a nightmarish experience. President Barack Obama did just that with the launch of his website, Fight the Smears, which immediately responds to untrue rumors and accusations. Campaign spokesperson Tammy Vietor explained that, "The Obama campaign isn't going to let dishonest smears spread across the Internet unanswered. Whenever challenged with these lies, we will aggressively push back with the truth and help our supporters debunk the false rumors floating around the Internet."[136] When Donald Trump called on Obama to provide his birth certificate— suggesting that Obama was not actually an American citizen—Obama used this site to post a scanned copy of his birth certificate.[137]

Another good tactic for fighting smears is the use of humor, especially in the form of YouTube response videos. After a negative remark from Conan O'Brien on the Tonight Show, Newark Mayor Cory Booker responded in a humorous YouTube video that highlighted the city's strong points, and (humorously) told Conan that he was on the "Newark New Jersey Airport no-fly list," ending with, "Try JFK, buddy".[138] If he hadn't responded, Conan's remarks could have stigmatized the city and mayor. By using humor in his response, however, Booker was able to spread some positive points about the city, while showing that he's

---

136   "Obama launches website against 'smears'", http://www.boston.com/news/politics/politicalintelligence/2008/06/obama_launches_4.html (accessed 27 June 2011).

137   "The Truth About Barack's Birth Certificate", Fight the Smears, http://www.fightthesmears.com/articles/5/birthcertificate (accessed 28 June 2011).

138   "Newark Mayor Cory Booker grounds Conan O'Brien with video jab", NJ.com, http://www.nj.com/news/index.ssf/2009/09/post_82.html (accessed 27 June 2011).

a good sport. He also came off as competent and serious, yet someone who could share a good laugh.

While engaging the opposition will likely never fully erase the damage of a pervasive smear, it can do a measure of good. Keeping things light, responding early, and not ignoring the problem can diffuse many political smears with before they get out of hand. Political campaigns can greatly benefit from using President Obama and Mayor Cory Booker as examples of ORM done right, while Representative Anthony Weiner is an excellent example of what not to do. In emulating these good examples, perhaps future campaigns can help further Obama's goal of "fighting the smears".

Keep your Online Watchdogs on the Alert

With the rise of social media platforms, it's been increasingly easy for opponents to use them as smear tools. Facebook, Twitter, and other social sites don't take sides. But whoever wins is usually in the driver's seat when it comes to the use of social networking tools.

One of the biggest social media debacles in politics was between Democratic Party candidate Attorney General Martha Coakley and Republican candidate Scott Brown.[139] Coakley lost, which many said was attributed to a "Twitter bomb" incident during the special election held to fill in the seat of the late Edward Kennedy in Massachusetts. Nine anonymous Twitter accounts were documented to be spreading rumors about Coakley taking money from health insurance lobbyists. The tweets included links to websites narrating details of the alleged 'take'. News spread virally for two hours before Twitter authorities took down the accounts, and the damage was done. People retweeted the

---

139   "When Campaigns Manipulate Social Media", 10 November 2010, http://www. theatlantic.com/politics/archive/2010/11/when-campaigns-manipulate-social-me-dia/66351/ (accessed 19 June 2011).

rumors over and over again on Twitterverse, further spreading the rumor and tarnishing the Coakley campaign.

Many experts say that the debacle could have been prevented if Coakley's campaign had digital watchdogs scoping out the other side. If they had caught wind of the rumors on Twitter much sooner and reported the incident, they could have stopped the smear and turned the tide on Election Day.

Suppressing Hostile Flash Mobs

In recent years and by evidence of the number of YouTube videos, flash mobs have been a powerful way to get people's attention. Flash mobs can be carefully pre-planned, coordinated, or choreographed— often through text messaging and other mobile technologies. Performers and participants often appear indistinguishable from a group of people in a public area, such as a college quad, department store, train station or other public square or park. Suddenly, at an appointed time, the flash mob emerges in a mass dance or performance to grab people's attention. Sometimes performances are sequenced— with a group divided into smaller groups that perform in a 'cascade', one after the other until all subgroups are performing simultaneously. In 2009, Oprah staged one of the biggest flash mobs in Chicago in which over 20,000 dancers took over Chicago's Michigan Avenue to the tune of the Black Eyed Peas' "I Gotta Feeling".

While flash mobs take place in the offline world, they are often created and organized through social networking, relying on people's social coordination on digital platforms. They are seemingly ephemeral, lasting only a couple of minutes— but the impact can be more permanent. The power of flash mobs is that they are usually captured and shared by spectators. People take out their cell phones and cameras and record the performance. Videos go up on YouTube or on blogs and websites— attracting thousands if not millions of viewers. These mock synchronous events are amplified and spread through social media, making them impossible to ignore. They can be a great way to draw attention to a campaign or cause.

Flash mobs are increasingly becoming a part of the political landscape, too. In Canada earlier this year, students at the University of Guelph in Ontario organized a 'vote mob' in time for the country's 41st general election.[140] Dubbed a 'surprise party' by organizers, similar vote mobs were organized on college campuses across the country. At least 200 people attended the Guelph flash mob event, which involved participants running out of a bush and holding up a banner that said, "Surprise! We are Voting!" The message was created in response to comedian Rick Mercer's call for young people to 'do the unexpected' and vote, a reference to the low voter turnout among people ages 18-24 in the last election. The Guelph organizer extolled the ability of flash mobs to call attention to important causes, saying that these groups inject a sense of playfulness to election campaigns often dominated by negativity.

Unfortunately, your opposition is also thinking the same thing and flash mobs can be used to disrupt your political rallies and events.

In 2009, German Chancellor Angela Merkel was confronted by a flash mob. Around a dozen flash mob participants in a crowd of about 2,000 in Hamburg, Germany held up signs and screamed sarcastic "Yeah's!" after every sentence in Merkel's speech.[141] In another event where Merkel gave a speech, a different flash mob responded with the same tactic of coordinated mockery and heckling. According to the flash mob organizers, the word spread like wildfire on blogs and social networking sites like Twitter. "Yeah" fans took their cues from their friends and online networks and were able to self-organize meet-ups at venues where Merkel spoke. The events were recorded and streamed live over the Internet and uploaded onto YouTube and viewed by almost 300,000 people.

---

140 "Vote mobs' shake up election", April 2011, http://www.cbc.ca/news/politics/canadavotes2011/story/2011/04/06/cv-election-flash-vote-mobs.html (accessed 29 June 2011).

141 "Flash Mobs Confront Merkel With Sarcastic 'Yeah!' Campaign", 9 September 2009, http://www.spiegel.de/international/germany/0,1518,650551,00.html (accessed 29 June 2011).

Another use of flash mobs as instrument of protest took place in Zurich, Switzerland. Greenpeace used the power of social media to organize a flash mob to draw attention to the dangers of nuclear power. It was targeted toward nuclear power suppliers and the government. The flash mob involved about 120 people who all simultaneously 'dropped dead' at 12:15 pm.[142] Spectators were shocked and scrambled to help the 'fallen' performers. *The message*: Switzerland was ill-prepared for a possible nuclear catastrophe at its plants around the country.

To prepare for possible flash mobs attacking your campaign guerilla-style, follow these tips:

1. Stay alert and monitor the online conversation.

The essence of flash mobs is that they are spontaneous, making them difficult to catch. But like all strategies, they need to be coordinated, organized, and promoted. Campaigns can usually catch a flash mob by listening and monitoring social media platforms. Check the Facebook and Twitter profiles of your opponent and see what supporters are buzzing about. If your campaign is holding an event in 'enemy' territory, keep your ears perked to hints of a possible flash mob staging itself at your event.

2. Dedicate staffers to patrol the perimeter of your event.

Telltale signs of a flash mob is about to start its performance are the coordinated checking of mobile phones by several people at once. Have your patrol keep a loose eye on this activity. Many times, it will be

---

142   "Ecology Awareness with Flash Mob Campaign", 25 May 2010, http://www.social-brand-value.com/2010/05/25/ecology-awareness-with-flash-mob-campaign/ (accessed 29 June 2011).

difficult to tell, but knowing when something is about to take place can give you some time to prepare— such as alerting authorities to arrive to escort protesters away. Practice care in organizing these crackdowns though. If you are caught on video being aggressive with protesters, it can cause a stir and risk your campaign being branded as aggressive or defensive.

3. Stay above the fray.

It happens. If the campaign is victimized by a flash mob, keep your cool. Mobilize quickly to escort people away, but don't be violent. Have a sense of humor about the experience. Flash mobs are meant to incite violent emotion and reaction— don't give your opponent the satisfaction of your campaign losing its cool or cracking down too hard. During the Wisconsin protests, Senator Ron Johnson made the mistake of calling what he saw of protesters taking over the legislature as "mob rule" and an example of "thuggery", trying to thwart electoral will. It made the GOP appear at odds with the fundamental right to assembly. Don't overreact. As soon as the 'performance' is over, keep to your messaging and finish that speech.

Conclusion

ONE DAY will we be declaring that it was Facebook that won it? Or Twitter that tipped it? Many political trends have come and gone throughout history but one thing is presently clear, that the internet and social media are becoming leading players in who gets elected. Once unfathomable in theory— such ideas, that the internet could sway an election would have been unthinkable just 5 years ago, as Facebook was still a toy being used only by university students to converse and Twitter didn't start until March 2006. But greater connectivity to one another, combined with the ability to reach tens of millions of voters, with the single click of a button, has leveled the playing field and over-all the modern election process. Greater uses of these technologies will only become more prevalent, begging the ultimate question "Will we see people get elected in the future, just based upon internet notoriety"?

Author Neil Postman was the first to call it in his controversial book Amusing Ourselves to Death. Back then Postman claimed we had moved from a print based (reading) society to an image based (television) society and the shift had resulted in a nation of people who have lost their desire and ability to think rationally. But while things are a bit different now, many things remain the same. Just as we witnessed with the introduction of televised debates a half century ago, social media has now become a key weapon in the battle for people's hearts, minds and votes, leaving those who ignore it to be left behind.

At the time Postman was writing about television— a far less pervasive form of technology than today's Internet or smart-phones. As we embrace this new world of technology we enter into a different place where communication has become far shorter. Emails indicate this, as does the Facebook status update and the infamous tweet. As we have seen Twitter is indicative of the new way people are talking to each other, think 140 characters or less. With new technology comes new language, new lingo and a new way of seeing the world as we now watch the inane, the nonsensical and the mundane become topics of conversation.

It all seems that once a forum is created for communication, communication will happen— regardless of the quality of the content, or substance begging the question. Was Postman's warning right when he stated, "To be unaware that a technology comes equipped with a program for social change, to maintain that technology is neutral, to make the assumption that technology is always a friend to culture is at this late hour, stupidity plain and simple. Moreover, we have seen enough by now to know that technological changes in our modes of communication are even more ideology-laden than changes in our modes of transportation. Introduce the alphabet to a culture and you change its cognitive habits, its social relations, its notions of community, history and religion. Introduce the printing press with movable type, and you do the same. Introduce speed-of-light transmission of images and you make a cultural revolution. Without a vote. Without polemics. Without guerrilla resistance. Here is ideology, pure if not serene. Here is ideology without words, and all the more powerful for their absence. All that is required to make it stick is a population that devoutly believes in the inevitability of progress. And in this sense all Americans are Marxists, for we believe nothing if not that history is moving us toward some preordained paradise and that technology is the force behind that movement."

There is no question that social media and its tentacles are slowly becoming interwoven into the fabric of our lives. As time continues the logos and names and websites currently utilized helping towards propelling a candidate into victory lane might change, but one thing is certain, social media and its influence on the political process is here to stay. As the next major elections loom, social media will play a greater role it their outcome. Are we ready for that? We may have to be.

CPSIA information can be obtained at www.ICGtesting.com
Printed in the USA
LVOW10s0305130514

385547LV00010B/120/P